WILLIAMSTOWN
VERMONT IN THE
CIVIL WAR

WILLIAMSTOWN
VERMONT IN THE
CIVIL WAR

PAUL G. ZELLER

THE History PRESS

Published by The History Press
Charleston, SC 29403
www.historypress.net

Front cover images courtesy of the Williamstown Historical Society and the U.S. Army Military Institute. Back cover image courtesy of the Vermont Historical Society.

First published 2010

Manufactured in the United States

ISBN 978.1.59629.690.9

Library of Congress Cataloging-in-Publication Data

Zeller, Paul G., 1946-
Williamstown, Vermont, in the Civil War / Paul G. Zeller.
p. cm.
Includes bibliographical references and index.
ISBN 978-1-59629-690-9
1. Williamstown (Vt. : Town)--History, Military--19th century. 2. Vermont--History--Civil War, 1861-1865--Registers. 3. United States--History--Civil War, 1861-1865--Registers. 4. Soldiers--Vermont--Williamstown (Town)--Registers. 5. Soldiers--Vermont--Williamstown (Town)--History--19th century. 6. Williamstown (Vt. : Town)--Genealogy. I. Title.
F59.W593Z45 2010
929'.374363--dc22
2010041893

CONTENTS

ACKNOWLEDGEMENTS

No one writes a book alone, and this book is no exception. I am indebted to a number of people. I would first like to thank my wife, Sally, who proofed the entire book several times, as well as taking a number of the photographs. The following members of the Williamstown Historical Society reviewed chapters of the book and helped gather photographs and family histories: Becky Watson, Stan and Carol Corneille, Ed and Joyce McGlynn, Larry Wiggin, Larry Ellison, Lila Walbridge and Irene Walbridge. Williamstown resident Gerald Hinckley reviewed the piece on Major Isaac Lynde. Thanks to my good friend Euclid D. Farnham, who reviewed portions of the book and gave me sound advice. Paul Carnahan and Marjorie Strong, of the Vermont Historical Society, were of great assistance in tracking down photographs and helping me with scanning. Flora O'Hara and Roberta Taylor of Williamstown's Ainsworth Public Library happily supported this project. Special thanks to Kristen Hallett, Cliff Hersey, Dr. Carleton Young and Scott Benoir, descendants of Williamstown soldiers, who freely shared family information and photographs. Thanks to Prudence Dougherty of the University of Vermont's Special Collections for allowing me to use one of their photographs. Thanks to John Gibson for allowing me to use one of the photographs from his collection. Lastly, thanks to Debbie Palmer, town clerk of Williamstown, and Barbara Graham, assistant town clerk, who gave me free access to the records in the town vault and were not only helpful but also always patient with me.

INTRODUCTION

This is a book I never intended to write. I was asked by the president of our historical society to revise our town's history book in the fall of 2008, and in the process I started finding a lot of information on Williamstown men in the Civil War. I decided I could not put all the Civil War information in the revision of the town's history book, so I decided to put it in a book of its own. This book includes men who enlisted in Williamstown, Williamstown natives who served in other state units or the regular army and veterans from other places who settled in Williamstown after the war. As much as possible, it follows the men from birth to death.

I have strived to be as accurate as possible. That means that not all the stories are heroic. For this I do not apologize. These were common, ordinary men. Some were heroes and some were not, and most were probably somewhere in the middle. Some of the men joined the military to defend the Union, others joined for adventure and still others, later in the war, joined for the large cash bounties that were being offered.

I have made every effort to ensure that this book is historically accurate, and I accept full responsibility for any inaccuracies that may be found. I truly hope this work does justice to the records and memory of these men and that all citizens of Williamstown will be proud of them.

All proceeds from this book will go to the Williamstown Historical Society.

1
THE HISTORY OF THE WILLIAMSTOWN SOLDIERS' MONUMENT

The history of the Williamstown Civil War Soldiers' Monument is, unfortunately, not a very pretty story. From its conception to its erection, it was surrounded by controversy, squabbling and hard feelings.

At the annual town meeting held on March 3, 1868, the town voted to raise money, not to exceed $2,000, for a monument to the memory of the officers and soldiers who counted against Williamstown's quota in the Civil War and were killed in battle, died of wounds or died of disease. It was also voted that a committee of three be appointed to oversee the design, construction and erection of the monument. John Lynde, Daniel Martin and Septa Simons were chosen as the committee members.

During the annual town meeting of March 2, 1869, it was voted to have the soldiers' monument located on land in front of Enos F. Walker's house, the house to the right of today's Burrell Roofing Co.; however, considerable resentment lingered over where the monument would be located, and a special town meeting was held on March 31 to settle the question. During this meeting, Williamstown citizens voted to locate the monument on the grounds of the Baptist meetinghouse. Again, the matter was settled, or so it would seem.

Only a little over two weeks had gone by before another town meeting was held on April 17 concerning the soldiers' monument. In an attempt to clear the air, it was voted to rescind all votes taken on the monument since the annual town meeting held in March 1868. Next, it was voted to pass on article three, which asked if the town would vote to build a tomb in the

The Williamstown Soldiers' Monument decorated for Decoration Day, circa 1880. *Courtesy of the Williamstown Historical Society.*

village cemetery and locate the soldiers' monument there. Also, articles four and five were dismissed. Article four asked if the monument could be placed in front of the town hall. Article five asked if the town would vote to sell the monument. It was finally voted to locate the monument on the grounds of what is today Williamstown's United Federated Church.

On June 12, another special town meeting was held. Article two, which asked if the town would vote to place the monument in front of the town hall, and article three, which asked to locate the monument in the village cemetery, were both dismissed. By this time, Septa Simons had had enough and asked to be excused from the committee. It was voted that Simons be excused and that Nathan Hall replace him.

The monument, made by the Colby and Walker Company of Montpelier, was erected in October 1870 where it stands today between the Williamstown Historical Society and the United Federated Church. The cost of the monument was $1,775, and the cast-iron fence that surrounds it cost $225. The monument consists of a granite base with a twenty-five-foot-high marble obelisk topped by an eagle with outstretched wings. On the obelisk are carved the names of seventeen Williamstown men who died for their country. Resentment on both sides of the monument's location controversy was so strong that there does not appear to have been a dedication ceremony. After one more unsuccessful attempt by some to have the monument moved, the controversy was apparently finally over, as nothing more can be found in the town records.[1]

2

1ST VERMONT INFANTRY REGIMENT

The 1st Vermont was the first regiment raised in Vermont at the outbreak of the Civil War. It was raised in response to a nationwide call from President Lincoln for seventy-five thousand troops to serve for three months. It was thought that the rebellion could be put down in that amount of time. The companies of the 1st Vermont reported to their camp of instruction in Rutland, Vermont, on or about May 2, 1861. The regiment was mustered into U.S. service on May 8 and left the next day for Fort Monroe in Hampton, Virginia, where it arrived on May 13. On May 26, the Vermonters moved a few miles east of Fort Monroe to the tip of the Virginia Peninsula known as Newport News, overlooking the James River and Hampton Roads.

The only combat experienced by the Vermonters was the calamitous attack on a Confederate outpost at Big Bethel, eight miles north of Fort Monroe. Several Federal columns left Fort Monroe at about 1:00 a.m. on June 10 using several roads. They were to rendezvous at a road intersection about three miles south of the Confederate position and make a surprise attack. In the dark, the Federals mistook one another for Rebels and fired into one another's columns. Not only was the element of surprise removed from their attack, but also 2 men were killed and 21 wounded. Even though it was apparent that the Confederates knew they were coming, the Federals decided to continue. In a poorly managed attack, the Federal force of 4,400 men was defeated by 1,408 Rebels. The Federals lost 76 men, while the Confederates lost only 11. The Vermonters lost 1 man killed. The 1st Vermont returned to Brattleboro on August 7 and was mustered out of service on August 15.[2]

Ai Brown

Company F

Ai Brown enlisted in Company F, 1st Vermont Infantry Regiment, in Williamstown on May 2, 1861. At the time, he was unmarried and was working as a farmer. Brown was mustered out of service, with the rest of his regiment, on August 15, 1861. He returned to Williamstown and the next month enlisted in Company F, 1st Regiment, U.S. Sharpshooters, on September 11, 1861 (see p. 139).[3]

Charles E. Davis

Company F

Charles E. Davis enlisted in Company F, 1st Vermont Infantry Regiment, in Williamstown on May 2, 1861, at age twenty. He was mustered out of service on August 15, 1861. He died on May 26, 1917, at Fort Lupton, Colorado.[4]

Henry W. Davis

Company F

Henry W. Davis was born on October 15, 1835. He enlisted in Company F, 1st Vermont Infantry Regiment, in Williamstown on May 2, 1861. He was mustered out of service with his regiment on August 15, 1861. He enlisted in Company D, 12th Vermont Infantry Regiment, on August 23, 1862 (see p. 109).[5]

Charles E. Peters

Company D

Charles E. Peters, son of William and Mary Johnson Peters, was born in Boston, Massachusetts, on August 24, 1834. He enlisted in Company D, 1st Vermont Infantry Regiment, on May 2, 1861. At the time, he was living in Manchester, New Hampshire. He was mustered out of service with the regiment on August 15, 1861. He enlisted in Company D, 8th Vermont Infantry Regiment, on January 29, 1862 (see p. 75).[6]

3
FIRST VERMONT BRIGADE

The Vermont Brigade was one of the most famous units in the Civil War, and it had the reputation of being one of the hardest-fighting and fastest-marching brigades in the Army of the Potomac. In the vicious Battles of the Wilderness and Spotsylvania, from May 5 to May 18, 1864, it lost 1,645 of its 2,800 officers and men.

The idea of the Vermont Brigade was first suggested by Brigadier General William F. Smith to the commander of the Army of the Potomac, Major General George B. McClellan, in the fall of 1861. At that time, it was against War Department policy to brigade regiments of the same state together. The fear was that if a brigade made up of regiments from different states suffered a heavy loss, it would spread the impact over a large geographical area and would not upset the general population as much. It was also felt that rivalry between the regiments would improve efficiency.

In spite of War Department policy, McClellan allowed Smith to create a Vermont Brigade consisting of the 2nd, 3rd, 4th and 5th Vermont Infantry Regiments. The brigade was rounded out on October 24, 1861, with the arrival of the 6th Vermont.

At the outbreak of the Civil War, William F. Smith was serving as a captain in the regular army. With the formation of the 3rd Vermont, the governor of Vermont chose Smith, who was a Vermonter, as its commander, and he was promoted to colonel of volunteers. Smith joined the 3rd Vermont at its camp at Chain Bridge in Arlington, Virginia, during the last week of July. Smith was soon put in command of all regiments in and around the vicinity of Chain Bridge, which consisted of the 2nd Vermont, 6th Maine and 33rd New York, as well as several other units. On August 13, 1861, Colonel Smith was promoted to brigadier general. It was around this time that Smith approached McClellan about the formation of a Vermont Brigade. Before the Vermont Brigade was fully formed, Smith was given division command, and newly promoted Brigadier General William T.H. Brooks, an 1841 West Point graduate from Ohio, became the brigade's commander.

The Vermont Brigade was officially the First Brigade of Smith's Division but always retained the name the "Vermont Brigade." In the spring of 1862, just prior to the launching of the Army of the Potomac's Peninsula Campaign, the army was reorganized into corps, and the Vermont Brigade was designated the Second Brigade of the Second Division of the Fourth Corps, but again it was unofficially referred to as the Vermont Brigade. On May 18, 1862, McClellan again reorganized his army, and the Vermont Brigade became the Second Brigade of the Second Division of the Sixth Corps.

In its four years of service, the Vermont Brigade fought in every major battle with the Army of the Potomac: Savage Station, Crampton's Gap, Antietam, First Fredericksburg, Second Fredericksburg, Gettysburg, the Wilderness, Spotsylvania, Cold Harbor and Petersburg. In the summer of 1864, the Sixth Corps was sent to Washington, D.C., to protect the capital from an attack by Lieutenant General Jubal A. Early. After that was successfully accomplished, the Sixth Corps, along with the Vermont Brigade, was attached to the newly organized Army of the Shenandoah, under the command of Major General Philip H. Sheridan, and participated in the Battles of Winchester, Fisher's Hill and Cedar Creek. In December, the Sixth Corps rejoined the Army of the Potomac at Petersburg. The Vermont Brigade fought in the final breakthrough at Petersburg and in the last major action of the Army of the Potomac at Sailor's Creek. The Vermont Brigade ceased to exist when its regiments were mustered out of service in the summer of 1865.[7]

4
2nd VERMONT INFANTRY REGIMENT

The 2nd Vermont was recruited about the time the 1st Vermont was on its way south. It was mustered into service in Burlington on June 20, 1861. On June 24, the regiment shipped out for Washington, D.C. After several days' stay in the nation's capital, the Vermonters moved across the Potomac to Alexandria, Virginia. Here they spent several weeks on picket duty and practicing to become soldiers. The Vermonters moved with the rest of the army on July 17, 1861, toward Manassas, where the Federal army and the Confederates collided on July 21. The 2nd Vermont was one of the last units to enter the fray and soon had to retreat to Washington with the rest of the army. After the humiliating defeat at Bull Run, President Lincoln placed Major General George B. McClellan in charge of the Army of the Potomac, which was camped around Washington. For the rest of the fall and winter, McClellan shaped his 100,000 men into an efficient army. The 2nd Vermont was incorporated into the Vermont Brigade in the fall of 1861 and fought with it for the rest of the war. It was mustered out of service on June 19, 1865.[8]

Camp of the 2nd Vermont Infantry Regiment at Camp Griffin, Virginia. Photograph by George H. Houghton. *Courtesy of the Vermont Historical Society.*

ORIGEN ALLAN BLANCHARD

Company D

Origen A. Blanchard, son of Hiram and Parthenia Mary Earle Blanchard, was born in Barre on December 17, 1838. He enlisted in Company D, 2nd Vermont Infantry Regiment, in Williamstown on September 7, 1861, and listed his occupation as a farmer. He was a small man, measuring only five feet, three and a half inches tall. During his service, he was promoted to corporal on August 28, 1862, and to sergeant on December 8, 1863. He was mustered out on September 20, 1864. After returning to Williamstown from the army, Origen resumed farming. He married Myrna L. Elmer, the daughter of George W. and Emeline Fowler Elmer, in Williamstown on September 19, 1867. They had two children: Leon R., born on August 25, 1870, and Hattie M., born on November 21, 1874. Origen received a small monthly government disability pension for chronic diarrhea, which he contracted in the army. He died in Williamstown on January 12, 1911, of heart disease, chronic diarrhea and rheumatism and was buried in Williamstown's Village Cemetery.[9]

John E. Clough

Company D

John E. Clough, the son of Clark E. and Maria M. Brown Clough, was born in Williamstown on January 7, 1841. After finishing his education, he moved to East Montpelier, where he farmed. He enlisted in Company D, 2nd Vermont Infantry Regiment, on September 7, 1861, in Montpelier at age twenty. At that time, he was a bachelor and stood five feet, six inches tall. He was wounded in the hand on June 29, 1862, at the Battle of Savage Station. The bullet struck him just above the first joint of the middle finger of his left hand, removing that part of his finger. Later, the rest of his injured finger was amputated. He reenlisted in the army on January 31, 1864, and received a $300 bounty from Williamstown. On May 10, 1864, Clough was captured at the Battle of Spotsylvania and was sent to the prisoner of war camp at Andersonville, Georgia. He escaped from Andersonville with several other prisoners on January 10, 1865, and they made their way back to Union lines. During his captivity, he contracted scurvy, rheumatism and neuralgia. He was mustered out of service on July 15, 1865.

John E. Clough, Company D, 2nd Vermont Infantry Regiment. *Courtesy of Cliff Hersey.*

John Clough married Laura E. Andrews on November

10, 1873, in Waitsfield, Vermont. She was born on October 24, 1854, in Duxbury, Vermont, and was the daughter of Ethan and Jane Andrews. They lived in East Montpelier from 1865 to 1870 and then in Barre from 1870 to 1882. Then they moved back to East Montpelier. Laura left John about 1900. According to Laura's brother, George, "Her husband was a man that drank to excess, and when under the influence of liquor, abused his wife shamefully. She could not endure ill treatment and about 25 years ago she left him, and they have never lived together since that time." Laura's cousin Melvin A. Hoadley (his mother and Laura's mother were sisters) stated, "Her husband was a man that used to drink intoxicating liquor, and at times to excess, and at such times abused his wife, striking her, and otherwise tormenting her." Laura first moved in with her father in Moretown. She then returned to Montpelier and moved in with her daughter Myrtie J. Clough.

By 1924, John Clough was in his early eighties and was living by himself in East Montpelier. Between 8:00 and 8:30 a.m. on June 19, his housekeeper found him lying on the floor in his house with his throat bleeding. She rushed to notify neighbors, who called a physician from Montpelier and the jail, from where Deputy Sheriff Ralph Mears was sent to the scene.

When the doctor arrived, he found that Clough had cut his own throat with a jackknife. The wound was a slash over two inches long and so deep that it punctured his windpipe, but he was still alive. He was rushed to the Heaton Hospital but passed away about three hours after arriving.

He was conscious up to a minute or so before he died at the hospital and was able to speak, but he said nothing about what had happened. After a preliminary investigation, authorities stated that it was apparent it was a case of suicide. A large jackknife with a blade about four inches long was found near his bed and was believed to have been the knife Clough used to end his life. There were no signs of a struggle, and the only other mark Mr. Clough received besides the one in the neck was a very slight cut on the left forefinger. As far as was known, he had no enemies, and fifty dollars in cash was found in his pocket.

Relatives and friends could not find any reason for his committing suicide, as he had not been despondent about anything and had no financial or other worries. One can only wonder if he had not, for years, been suffering from what we now know as post-traumatic stress disorder.

Besides his wife, Laura, he was survived by his two daughters, Miss Myrtie Clough and Mrs. Bernard Hersey, both of Montpelier. John E. Clough was buried at the Cutler Cemetery in East Montpelier. Laura Clough died on March 13, 1931.[10]

Thomas Clury

Company F

Thomas Clury was born in Williamstown. On May 7, 1861, the twenty-year-old farmer enlisted in Company F, 2nd Vermont Infantry Regiment, in Williamstown and was selected as a corporal. He was slightly wounded at the Battle of Bull Run on July 21, 1862. He was promoted to sergeant on August 6, 1863. Clury served the rest of his three-year commitment without a scratch and was mustered out on June 29, 1864.[11]

Ralph Ditty

Company F

Ralph Ditty, son of William and Emily Chaffee Ditty, enlisted in Company F, 2nd Vermont Infantry Regiment, in Roxbury, Vermont, on May 7, 1861. The twenty-year-old farmer stood five feet, eight and a half inches tall and had blue eyes.

The Vermont Brigade was up early on November 9, 1862, marching down the Warrenton Turnpike to New Baltimore, Virginia. During the march, the 2nd Vermont, along with several other units under the command of Brigadier General Francis L. Vinton, was detailed as the division rear guard. While slogging through the deep mud between White Plains and New Baltimore, Vinton happened along and told the Vermonters to move more quickly. Private Ralph Ditty took exception to the order. Ditty had fallen back about six paces from the rest of his group and had caught the general's attention. In Vinton's words:

> *I took pains on the way to close up all stragglers…When I first noticed the conduct of the prisoner* [Ditty] *as being insubordinate, I was urging up some stragglers belonging to the rear guard and not addressing him (the prisoner) he in an insolent tone said you can't make us go any faster than we can and you can't ride us down much or words to that effect. This called my attention to the prisoner. I saw he was a little behind his guard, so I rushed my horse toward him and ordered him to close up. He jumped to one side, clubbed his piece and lifted it over his shoulder in a threatening attitude to strike. The moment he threatened I checked my horse and dropped the point*

> *of my sword to run him through if he did strike and at that moment with a laugh, he stepped into his guard.*

Ditty was brought before a court-martial on November 19. He was charged with two specifications in violation of the ninth article of war, which, in short, authorized the execution of any officer or soldier who would strike, draw or lift a weapon or threaten violence to a superior officer. The first specification was for speaking disrespectfully to a superior officer and the second for threatening a superior officer. At the trial, Ditty's description of the confrontation in the muddy road that day differed from Vinton's. Ditty stated:

> *The first I knew of his being an officer he rode his horse close onto me and ordered me to close up. I said I was closing up as fast as I could. He kept along side, his horse pretty close to me. I had to step to one side. He drew his sword at this time and struck at me. He said close up again. I said give me a chance. I walked into the ranks as fast as I could. He ordered the Lieut. of the guard to take my name and have me court martialed. As I stepped out to one side of the road, I had to catch hold of my musket with both hands and at the same time, keep his horse off me. I did not attempt to strike the officer at all.*

Witnesses for Ditty corroborated Ditty's statement, but the court found him guilty of the two specifications. He was not, however, found guilty of violating the ninth article of war. He was sentenced to forfeiture of a half month's pay for three months, and he had to memorize the ninth article of war and repeat it verbatim to his first sergeant. Considering this was a case of a private's word against that of a general's, this was a fairly mild punishment.

Ralph Ditty was wounded on May 3, 1863, at the Second Battle of Fredericksburg. He was mustered out of the army on June 29, 1864, at the expiration of his service. After his discharge, Ditty returned home to Roxbury. He married Laura S. Smith of Williamstown on March 8, 1866. They lived for five years in Northfield before moving to Williamstown. Ralph and Laura had three children: Clayton R., Winsor and Ernest L. Ralph received a government disability pension for chronic diarrhea, measles and lung disease he contracted in the army. Ralph Ditty died on November 8, 1901, at age sixty-eight of cerebral softening and was buried at Williamstown's Village Cemetery. Laura died on December 16, 1920, and was buried beside her husband.[12]

Leonard George

Company F

Leonard George enlisted in Company F, 2nd Vermont Infantry Regiment, in Williamstown on August 25, 1862. No record exists of him after he was mustered into service on October 2, 1862.[13]

Francis S. Martin

Company F

Francis S. Martin, son of Chester and Audeia W. Hill Martin, enlisted in Randolph, Vermont, on September 17, 1863, as a substitute for George W. Chandler, a Randolph native who was eligible for the upcoming draft. At the time of his enlistment, Martin was a twenty-nine-year-old farmer and a bachelor. He stood five feet, five and three-quarters inches tall and had gray eyes and brown hair. In addition to getting the bounty Randolph was paying, he got an additional $300 from the man for whom he substituted. After he was mustered into the army, he was sent south to join the 2nd Vermont Infantry Regiment. Upon his arrival at camp, Martin was assigned to Company F.

Francis Martin was slightly wounded in the neck in the Battle of the Wilderness on May 5, 1864, but was soon back with his regiment. On October 19, 1864, during the Battle of Cedar Creek, Martin was wounded again, only this time it was serious. As the enemy was pushing the Union line back, Martin stopped and rendered first aid to a fallen comrade. Just as he started off to rejoin his company, he was struck by a Minié ball in the left leg about two inches above the ankle joint. Because the bones were so badly broken, his leg had to be amputated several days later. The amputation was performed five and a half inches below the knee joint. After he was stabilized, he was evacuated back to Sloan General Hospital in Montpelier. He was not discharged from the hospital until August 25, 1865.

After Martin returned home to Williamstown on a wooden leg, he went back to farming with his father. (Today, the Martin house is the brick portion of the Gardens retirement facility.) Before leaving the hospital, he applied for a government pension, which he received, backdated to August 25, 1865, for eight dollars a month. On October 11, 1865, Francis and his

Francis S. Martin, Company F, 2nd Vermont Infantry Regiment, displaying his wound to the U.S. Pension Bureau. *Courtesy of Special Collections, University of Vermont.*

father were digging a hole beside a large boulder in one of their fields in order to bury it. Having done all they deemed safe, they left the field to get other tools to complete the job. For some reason, Francis returned and started digging under the boulder by himself. When he did not return as soon as was expected, his mother became alarmed and sent someone for him. He was found in the hole dead with the boulder on top of him, only his head and shoulders protruding. His body and limbs were completely crushed, and it took two hours to extricate him. He was buried at Williamstown's West Hill Cemetery.[14]

JOSEPH A. SANDERS

Company F

Joseph A. Sanders, son of Henry A. and Martha Lawson Sanders, was born in Middlesex, Vermont, on June 9, 1840. He enlisted in Company F, 2nd Vermont Infantry Regiment, in Montpelier on May 7, 1861, and was with the regiment in all its battles, from first Bull Run to Gettysburg. Then he was assigned as an orderly on the staff of General Lewis A. Grant, commander of the Vermont Brigade. He remained in that position until the close of the war. Private Sanders reenlisted on December 21, 1863. He married Diantha B. Williams on January 25, 1864, in Montpelier while he was home on his reenlistment furlough. Sanders was mustered out of service on July 15, 1865.

After the war, they moved to Williamstown, where he farmed. They had two children: Minnie E., born on August 23, 1866, and Perley G., born on October 28, 1873. Joseph received a small government pension for various ailments contracted in the army. He died on April 3, 1906, of heart disease and was buried at Williamstown's Village Cemetery. Diantha received a veteran widow's pension after Joseph's death. She died on November 8, 1920, of heart disease and was buried beside her husband.[15]

Eldon A. Tilden

Company D

Eldon A. Tilden, son of Lester and Rebekah Tilden, was born in Barre, Vermont. He enlisted in Company D, 2nd Vermont Infantry Regiment, in Barre on May 7, 1861, at age twenty-one and was selected as sergeant. Later, he was promoted to first sergeant of Company D, and then on November 20, 1863, he was promoted to second lieutenant in Company D. Tilden was mustered out of service on June 29, 1865. After the war, Tilden married Lucy Lynde of Williamstown. Lucy died on November 28, 1875, at age thirty-

Eldon A. Tilden, Company D, 2nd Vermont Infantry Regiment. *Courtesy of the Williamstown Historical Society.*

one, of Bright's disease and was buried at Williamstown's Village Cemetery. Next, Eldon married Mary A. Lake in Franklin Falls, New Hampshire, on September 17, 1879; it was the second marriage for both of them. They resided for the rest of their lives in Boston, Massachusetts, where Eldon was a merchant. He received a small government disability pension for chronic diarrhea, which he contracted in the army. Eldon died on August 30, 1885, of liver cancer and was buried at Williamstown's Village Cemetery.[16]

CHARLES A. WHITE JR.

Company D

Charles A. White enlisted in Company D, 2nd Vermont Infantry Regiment, in Williamstown on May 7, 1861, and was selected as corporal. He was admitted to the E Street Infirmary in Washington, D.C., on September 11, 1861, with bilious fever. While in the hospital he was reduced to private on October 1, 1861. The reduction in rank stemmed from the refusal of White and about 150 members of the 2nd Vermont to go on a night march on September 28. The noncommissioned officers were busted to the ranks, and the privates were thrown into the guardhouse for several weeks. White was wounded in the right knee at the Battle of Fredericksburg on December 13, 1862. White was mustered out on June 29, 1864, at the expiration of his enlistment. He enlisted again a month later on August 30, 1864, in Company C, 8th Vermont Infantry Regiment (see p. 81).[17]

5

3RD VERMONT INFANTRY REGIMENT

The 3rd Vermont Infantry Regiment was mustered into service on July 16, 1861, in St. Johnsbury, Vermont. The regiment moved south on July 24 and reached Washington, D.C., on the morning of July 26. A colonel for the regiment had not yet been found, and the men were under the command of the regiment's lieutenant colonel, Breed N. Hyde. The 3rd moved to Camp Lyon in Arlington, Virginia, where its mission was to guard the Chain Bridge. The regiment's colonel, William F. Smith, joined the regiment during the last week of July 1861. Smith was put in command of all regiments in and around the vicinity of the Chain Bridge, which consisted of the 2nd Vermont, 6th Maine and 33rd New York, along with several other units. On August 13, 1861, Colonel Smith was promoted to brigadier general, and Lieutenant Colonel Hyde was promoted to colonel of the 3rd Vermont.

Colonel Hyde resigned on January 15, 1863, and Thomas O. Seaver replaced him. Seaver remained in command until July 27, 1864, when he and the men whose terms of service were up went home. The remainder of the 3rd Vermont under the command of Major Horace W. Floyd was mustered out of service on July 11, 1865.[18]

JOHN W. BACON

Company E

John W. Bacon was born on April 12, 1836, in Medina, New York. Exactly when he moved to Williamstown is not known, but he married Sarah J. Stevens, of Chelsea, Vermont, in Williamstown on November 16, 1860. They were married by Reverend James S. Spinney of the Williamstown Methodist Church. The Bacons lived in Williamstown, where John was a farmer. They had two children: Frank E., born on September 6, 1864, and Artie E., born on March 17, 1871. On November 12, 1861, at age twenty-five, Bacon enlisted in Company E, 3rd Vermont Infantry Regiment, in Williamstown. He spent the winter of 1861–62 with his regiment at Camp Griffin on the outskirts of Washington, D.C. In the spring, Bacon's regiment, along with the rest of the Army of the Potomac, participated in the Peninsula Campaign on the Virginia Peninsula in an attempt to capture Richmond. In June, while building a bridge across the Chickahominy Swamp below Richmond, Bacon was pinned between two logs. The logs caught him in the lower abdomen and lower back, doing severe damage to his bladder. He was hospitalized and given a disability discharge from the army on October 31, 1862. He returned to Williamstown. On September 17, 1864, after recovering from his injuries, he enlisted in Company E, 8th Vermont Infantry Regiment (see p. 65).[19]

WILLIAM HARRISON HAMILTON

Company K

William H. Hamilton was born in Manchester, England. When he immigrated to the United States and how he ended up in Williamstown are not known; however, he enlisted in Company K, 3rd Vermont Infantry Regiment, in Williamstown on July 10, 1861. He was mustered out of service on July 27, 1864. Hamilton drowned in the Connecticut River in Brattleboro in the summer of 1896. It was suspected that he committed suicide, as he was considered "somewhat crazy." In February 1897, a young man admitted to finding Hamilton's gold watch near where the body was discovered. This led to an investigation by Hamilton's comrades in the Grand Army of the Republic, who at first suspected foul play but finally concluded that Hamilton had, in fact, committed suicide.[20]

Alden Slack

Company I

Alden Slack, son of James F. Slack, was born in Albany, Vermont, on March 20, 1838. He enlisted in Company I, 3rd Vermont Infantry Regiment, in Washington, Vermont, on July 5, 1861, and listed his occupation as a farmer. He reenlisted on December 21, 1863, and received a $100 bounty. He was wounded on May 5, 1864, in the Battle of the Wilderness and was slightly wounded again in the right knee on September 19, 1864, in the Battle of Winchester, Virginia. He was wounded a third and final time on October 19, 1864, at the Battle of Cedar Creek, Virginia. This time, the wound was serious. A Rebel Minié ball hit him in the right eye, destroying the eyeball before passing out through the side of his head. He spent two weeks in a field hospital in Winchester, Virginia, before being transferred to Camden Street Hospital in Baltimore, Maryland, where he remained for a month. Next, he was evacuated to Sloan General Hospital in Montpelier, where he was finally given a disability discharge on June 12, 1865. After the war, Slack resided in Chelsea, Vermont, where he married Hattie G. McAllister on January 24, 1868. Some time later, they moved to Williamstown. They had five children: Gertrude M., Archibald E., Mary I., Fannie F. and Victor E. Alden died on June 6, 1902, in South Royalton, Vermont, and was buried at Williamstown's Village Cemetery.[21]

Alden Slack, Company I, 3rd Vermont Infantry Regiment, displaying his eye wound to the U.S. Pension Bureau. *Courtesy of the National Archives.*

6
4th Vermont Infantry Regiment

The 4th Vermont Infantry Regiment was mustered into service at Camp Baxter, Brattleboro, Vermont, on September 21, 1861, and left for Washington, D.C., that evening. The regiment's colonel was Edwin H. Stoughton. The Vermonters arrived in Washington on September 23. On September 28, the 4th Vermont was sent to Chain Bridge in Arlington, Virginia, where it joined the 2nd, 3rd and 5th Vermont Regiments. There it spent the rest of the winter of 1861–62. The 4th Vermont was mustered out of service on June 19, 1865. In its four years of service, the 4th Vermont fought in every major battle with the Army of the Potomac, not to mention numerous skirmishes.[22]

Truman E. Blodgett

Company B

Truman E. Blodgett, the son of Heman and Sabina Blodgett of Williamstown, enlisted in Company B, 4th Vermont Infantry Regiment, in Williamstown on August 24, 1861. At the time, he was a nineteen-year-old bachelor living with his parents and helping his father run the family farm. He served honorably and was mustered out on September 30, 1864, at the expiration of his service. Truman Blodgett died on May 28, 1866, at age twenty-seven and was buried at the East Brookfield Cemetery. He was never married.[23]

Charles H. Knapp (alias Lewis Belknap)

Company B

Charles H. Knapp was born in Williamstown. He enlisted in Company B, 4th Vermont Infantry Regiment, in Williamstown on September 21, 1861. It is not known why he enlisted as Lewis Belknap. At the time of his enlistment, he listed his occupation as farmer. He was wounded on September 14, 1862, at the Battle of Crampton's Gap in Burkittsville, Maryland. Union forces were trying to clear Confederate troops out of the gap. Before the Vermont Brigade could climb the mountain to the gap, Confederate cavalry had to be flushed from behind a stone wall at the mountain's base. It was here that Knapp was wounded. He was hit on the left side of his head by a Minié ball. The ball grazed his scalp about two inches above his ear, leaving a four-inch cut. Knapp was in the process of ramming home a round in his rifle when he was hit. Putting his hand up to the wound, he remarked, "By thunder, if my head had been a little bigger they'd have got me that time." He continued firing his rifle and refused to leave the field. He was wounded again on December 13, 1862, at the Battle of Fredericksburg, Virginia. He had been ordered by his lieutenant to help a severely wounded comrade to the rear. While doing as ordered, he was hit by a Minié ball in the right leg. The bullet entered his thigh just below the hip joint and exited just above his knee, but fortunately no bones were broken. After recovering from this wound, he was transferred to Sixth Corps headquarters on light duty. Knapp reenlisted on December 15, 1863, and served honorably until mustered out of the army on July 13, 1865.

Apparently, Knapp did not suffer too much from his leg wound. In October 1882, he rode his bicycle from Montpelier through the Williamstown Gulf to East Randolph in "just a trifle over two hours." He married Mary Byron on June 29, 1887, in Littleton, New Hampshire. She was born in Canada and was formerly married to Oliver Byron, who died on April 14, 1884. From the records, it is apparent that neither Charles nor Mary was literate. Charles died of dysentery on September 6, 1904, in Peacham, Vermont. After Charles's death, Mary applied for a widow's pension. That is when she found out he had enlisted under another name. Thankfully, she was able to supply enough documentation to the Pension Bureau that she was awarded a twelve-dollar-a-month government widow's pension. Mary Knapp died on April 20, 1913.[24]

Newell Carleton

Company B

Nineteen-year-old Newell Carleton, son of Timothy and Lovisa Glidden Carleton, enlisted in Company B, 4th Vermont Infantry Regiment, in Williamstown on August 20, 1861, and was selected as a corporal. He died of disease at Camp Griffin in Arlington, Virginia, on November 17, 1861. He has either a gravestone or a cenotaph at Maplewood Cemetery in Barre, Vermont.[25]

Erastus Church

Company E

Erastus Church was born in 1817 in Springfield, New Hampshire. He married Jane Lull on March 4, 1850, in Granville, Vermont. They had one child, a son named Melvin E. Church. On December 5, 1863, at age forty-six, Erastus Church enlisted in Company E, 4th Vermont Infantry Regiment, in Granville, Vermont. He was wounded on September 19, 1864, at the Battle of Winchester, Virginia, where he was hit in the left hand by a Minié ball. The ball entered near where his third and fourth fingers joined his hand and exited near his wrist. It took a lot of bone and tendon with it as it went through his hand. After his wound healed, Church could never again fully straighten the fingers on his left hand. Church was mustered out of service on July 13, 1865. Sometime after his discharge from the army, the Churches moved to Williamstown. Apparently, Jane Church died before her husband because later in Erastus's life he was so senile that Williamstown resident George W. Savery, who served in the 1st Vermont Cavalry Regiment, was appointed as his guardian. On July 4, 1900, Erastus Church was admitted to the Vermont State Hospital for the Insane in Waterbury, Vermont, where he died on January 10, 1903, of a heart attack. He was buried in Williamstown's Village Cemetery.[26]

Chester Wright Clark

Company B

Chester W. Clark was born in Worcester, Vermont, on August 20, 1841. He enlisted in Company B, 4th Vermont Infantry Regiment, in Williamstown on August 26, 1861. He served with his regiment through the Peninsula and Antietam Campaigns without receiving a scratch, but his luck ran out on December 13, 1862, at the Battle of Fredericksburg. A Minié ball hit him in his left leg about six inches below the knee. It went through the calf, entered the right leg four inches below the knee and exited out the other side. After his wounds healed, he could only walk short distances and could not stand very long. Because of the effects of his wounds, he volunteered to serve in the Veteran Reserve Corps on September 1, 1864. He was the brother of Lewis L. Clark.

Chester Clark received a disability discharge at the end of his enlistment on September 20, 1864, and returned home to Williamstown. He married Mary A. Town Sanders on March 17, 1866, in Nashua, New Hampshire. She was the widow of Private Carlisle Sanders, Company D, 2nd Vermont Infantry Regiment. Mary Town and Carlisle Sanders had been married in Northfield on December 12, 1860. They resided in Berlin and had no children. Sanders was wounded on May 5, 1864, in the Battle of the Wilderness and died of his wounds on May 15, 1864. Mary received a government widow's pension after Sanders's death, until she married Chester. Chester and Mary had one child, Alfred Henry Clark, born on November 2, 1897. Sometime later, they moved to Chicago, where Chester was receiving a twenty-five-dollar-a month government pension because of his wounds. He died in Chicago on March 18, 1918. Mary died in Chicago on December 26, 1919.[27]

Lewis Leonard Clark

Company B

Lewis L. Clark was born in Worcester, Vermont, on November 30, 1836. Exactly when he and his brother Chester came to Williamstown is unknown, but he enlisted there in Company B, 4th Vermont Infantry Regiment, on August 20, 1861, at age twenty-five. He was wounded on December 13, 1862, at the Battle of Fredericksburg. Within a few days after he was wounded, Clark was evacuated to Patent Office Hospital in Washington, D.C. As soon as his father, John Clark, learned that Lewis had been wounded, he left for Washington. Unfortunately, Lewis died on January 13, 1863, before his father could reach him. John Clark brought his son's body back to Worcester, where Lewis was buried at Worcester's Village Cemetery. After John returned from Washington, he suffered from chronic diarrhea. He applied for a government pension about 1868 on the grounds that Lewis had been his sole support, but when inquiries were made by the Pension Bureau, it got no reply from John. John Clark died of cancer in Williamstown on September 21, 1870, and was buried at the village cemetery.[28]

FRANCIS B. COSGROVE

Company B

Francis B. Cosgrove was born in Williamstown. He enlisted in Company B, 4th Vermont Infantry Regiment, in Williamstown on September 12, 1861, at age twenty-four. He stood five feet, ten and a half inches tall with a light complexion, blue eyes and light hair. He listed his occupation as a butcher. In July 1862, as the Army of the Potomac lay in camp at Harrison's Landing a little below Richmond, Virginia, Cosgrove had diarrhea so bad that he was sent to the hospital at Fort Monroe in Hampton, Virginia. After recovering from diarrhea, he was sent to Vermont on recruiting duty. On December 20, 1863, his diarrhea grew worse again, and he started having heart problems. He was then sent to Camp Convalescent in Alexandria, Virginia, where he remained until he was given a disability discharge on April 8, 1863. Cosgrove applied for and received an eight-dollar-a-month government pension in 1863 for his heart disease and chronic diarrhea. By 1864, his health was so bad that he could not perform any manual labor. He married Millie Dorson (or Donson) in Nashua, New Hampshire, on May 13, 1871. They lived in Chelsea, Vermont, for a while after they were married, and he worked as a lumber dealer. In 1871, they lived in Ayer, New Hampshire. In 1872, they were living in Lowell, Massachusetts, where Francis died on June 6, 1872, of heart disease.[29]

Nelson C. Drew

Company K

Nelson C. Drew was born in Brandon, Vermont. He married Caroline Templeton on May 7, 1853, and they had a son born on August 7, 1856, whom they named Charles Henry Drew. In May 1857, Caroline left Nelson to live with another man. In September of that same year, she returned to live with Nelson, who apparently forgave her. By January 12, 1858, according to Nelson, Caroline's behavior had "become so outrageous" that he left her and their infant son. On August 9, 1859, Nelson and Caroline were divorced. Thirty-four-year-old Nelson Drew was living in Williamstown in 1863 when he was drafted on August 4. He was assigned to Company K, 4th Vermont Infantry Regiment. Three months later, on November 5, 1863, he died of typhoid fever in the regimental hospital in Warrenton, Virginia. The records are not clear about what happened to Caroline, but after Nelson's death Charles Drew was in the guardianship of an Amasa Macomber in Chesterfield, New York. Charles Drew was awarded a government pension until he turned sixteen years old.[30]

Willard Fay

Company B

Willard Fay was born in Calais, Vermont, on June 27, 1838. He enlisted in Company B, 6th Vermont Infantry Regiment, in Williamstown on August 26, 1861, at age twenty-four. He was mustered out of service on September 30, 1864. He died on July 19, 1900, of anemia and was buried at Robinson Cemetery in Calais.[31]

Frank M. Flint

Company B

Frank M. Flint was born in Williamstown in 1841. He enlisted in Company B, 4th Vermont Infantry Regiment, in Williamstown on September 3, 1861. At the time of his enlistment, he was a twenty-year-old wheelwright. He was given a disability discharge on February 10, 1862, for chronic diarrhea. Flint married Elizabeth D. Abbott on June 3, 1869, in Williamstown. Sometime around 1880, he became a railroad conductor on the Vermont Central Railroad. He died of kidney cancer on November 20, 1909, in Windsor, Vermont. His body was transported to Williamstown on November 22, and he was buried in Williamstown's Village Cemetery the next day.[32]

William J. Foster

Company B

William J. Foster was born in Williamstown on September 19, 1841. He enlisted in Company B, 4th Vermont Infantry Regiment, in Williamstown on August 26, 1861, and received a $315 town bounty. He was given a disability discharge on January 29, 1862, for heart trouble as a result of typhoid fever. After the war, Foster lived in East Montpelier, where he died on January 4, 1905, and was buried at the Cutler Cemetery.[33]

Reuben B. George

Company K

Reuben B. George was born in 1824. He married Lydia A. Boutwell on October 22, 1848, in Williamstown. They had two sons: Fred George, born on October 26, 1855, and Henry E. George, born on September 1, 1850. Both boys were born in Williamstown. Reuben George enlisted in Company K, 4th Vermont Infantry Regiment, on August 28, 1861. He died of chronic diarrhea in the U.S. Marine Hospital on Bedloe's Island (now site of the Statue of Liberty and called Liberty Island) in New York City Harbor on November 8, 1862. He was buried at Cypress Hill National Cemetery in Brooklyn, New York. He has a cenotaph at Riverside Cemetery in Killington, Vermont. Lydia received an eight-dollar-a-month government widow's pension backdated to November 8, 1862. She died on September 3, 1910.[34]

John G. Green

Company B

John G. Green was born in Williamstown. He enlisted in Company B, 4th Vermont Infantry Regiment, in Williamstown on August 26, 1861. He was mustered out of service on September 30, 1864. John Green died on November 12, 1878, and was buried at East Randolph Cemetery in East Randolph, Vermont.[35]

Joseph Gregory

Company K

Joseph Gregory, son of John Gregory, was born on March 21, 1832, in Cooperstown, New York. He enlisted in Company K, 4th Vermont Infantry Regiment, in Northfield, Vermont, on August 29, 1861, at age twenty-nine. He was wounded on July 12, 1864, at the Battle of Spotsylvania and was mustered out of service on September 30, 1864. He settled in Williamstown after the war and married Laura L. Cutting. Laura died of inflammation of the bowels on November 20, 1899, and was buried at Williamstown's Village Cemetery. Joseph died of heart disease on December 11, 1909, and was buried beside his wife.[36]

Jason Johnson

Company B

Jason Johnson, son of Hezikial and Nancy Horn Johnson, was born in Johnson, Vermont, on February 14, 1840. He enlisted in Company B, 4th Vermont Infantry Regiment, in Williamstown on August 22, 1862. Johnson received a slight wound on his right ear on September 14, 1862, at the Battle of Crampton's Gap, Maryland. He was mustered out of service on September 30, 1864. Jason Johnson enlisted in Company D, 1st Regiment, of Hancock's First Army Corps on January 23, 1865 (see p. 146).[37]

DEXTER M. JONES

Company B

Dexter M. Jones, the son of Emery and Inez Jones, was born on July 8, 1836, in Northfield, Vermont. He enlisted in Company B, 4th Vermont Infantry Regiment, in Williamstown on September 12, 1862, and was mustered out of service on September 30, 1864. After mustering out of the army, Jones returned to Williamstown. He married Catherine Sophia Staples, the daughter of John B. and Lucinda Staples of Williamstown, in Northfield on August 7, 1869. They had no children. When he got older, Dexter received a small government disability pension for chronic diarrhea he contracted in the army in 1861. In 1903, his pension was increased to seventeen dollars a month, and by his death it had been increased to thirty dollars a month. Dexter died on February 26, 1916, of heart trouble and was buried at Williamstown's Village Cemetery.[38]

CHARLES F. LAWRENCE

Company B

Charles F. Lawrence, son of William and Eliza Pierce Lawrence, was born in Fairlee, Vermont, on April 10, 1836. He first married Mary J. Wood in 1857. She died without bearing any children in 1859. He next married Eliza M. Dana in February 1861. With Eliza, he had four children: Mary J., Nellie E., Charles H. and William H. Lawrence enlisted in Company B, 4th Vermont Infantry Regiment, in Williamstown on August 21, 1861. At the time, he was farming in Williamstown. Lawrence served his three-year obligation and was mustered out of service on September 30, 1864, without ever being wounded. He did, however, contract a lung disease for which he received an eight-dollar-a-month government disability pension. Charles Lawrence died of heart disease on July 27, 1899, in Haverhill, New Hampshire, and was buried at Williamstown's Village Cemetery.[39]

Charles Lynde

Company B

Charles Lynde, son of Judge John and Polly Lynde, was born in Williamstown on September 7, 1842. He enlisted in Company B, 4th Vermont Infantry Regiment, in Williamstown on August 20, 1861, and was promoted to sergeant on November 1, 1862. At the expiration of his service, Lynde was mustered out on September 30, 1864. After his military service, Lynde returned to Williamstown, where he married Alice Martin on November 26, 1867. Charles Lynde died of smallpox on

Above: Alice Martin Lynde, wife of Charles Lynde. *Courtesy of the Williamstown Historical Society.*

Right: Postwar photograph of Charles Lynde, Company B, 4th Vermont Infantry Regiment. *Courtesy of the Williamstown Historical Society.*

November 14, 1872, at age thirty and was buried at Williamstown's Village Cemetery. Alice died at age thirty-six on October 15, 1880, and was buried beside her husband.[40]

FREDERICK MARCY LYNDE

Company B

Frederick M. Lynde, son of Isaac and Margaret Wight Lynde, was born on September 10, 1843, in Fiske, Wisconsin, where his father was stationed in the army. He returned to Williamstown and enlisted in Company B, 4th Vermont Infantry Regiment, on August 20, 1861. Soon after enlisting, Lynde was selected as a sergeant. He was promoted to second lieutenant on May 15, 1862. He resigned his commission on July 31, 1862, but later enlisted as a private in Company C, 1st Wisconsin Heavy Artillery, on August 18, 1863. In that unit, he was promoted to sergeant on February 17, 1865. Following in the footsteps of his father, Frederick Lynde was commissioned in the regular army as a second lieutenant in the 22nd U.S. Infantry Regiment on July 28, 1866 (see p. 149).[41]

WILLIAM HENRY MARTIN

Company B

William H. Martin, Company B, 4th Vermont Infantry Regiment. *Courtesy of John Gibson.*

William H. Martin, son of Chester and Audeia W. Hill Martin, was born in Williamstown on November 25, 1838. He enlisted in Company B, 4th Vermont Infantry Regiment, in Williamstown on August 19, 1861, at age twenty-two and was selected as the company's first sergeant. Martin was promoted to second lieutenant in Company A, 4th Vermont, on July 17, 1862. He was wounded in the Battle of Antietam, Maryland, on September 17, 1862, and was struck in the neck and left shoulder by a piece of shell at the Battle of Funkstown, Maryland, while pursuing Lee's army from Gettysburg on July 10, 1863. He was severely wounded at the Battle of the Wilderness on May 5, 1864, and died of those wounds on May 8, 1864. There is a stone at Williamstown's West Hill Cemetery that reads, "Wm. H. Martin died May 8th, 1864, 25 yrs. of age." It is probably a cenotaph.[42]

Eli Mayette

Company B

Eli Mayette was born in Canada and enlisted in Company B, 4th Vermont Infantry Regiment, in Williamstown on August 6, 1861. He was shot in the left shoulder at the Battle of Lee's Mill, Virginia, on April 16, 1862. After several months in the hospital, he returned to his regiment. At the Battle of Fredericksburg on December 13, 1862, a piece of shell hit his rifle, slamming the rifle into the right side of his groin and causing a hernia that put him back in the hospital, where he received a disability discharge. After his military service, Mayette returned to Canada, where he married Louisa C. Clemons on July 4, 1863, in Sutton. He was a twenty-eight-year-old widower, and Louisa was fifteen. Sometime later, they moved to Littleton, New Hampshire. Eli died on April 25, 1888, in Littleton, leaving Louisa with five children and no support. She applied for a veteran widow's pension, but it is unclear from the records if she received one.[43]

Dean Newcomb

Company B

Twenty-one-year-old Dean Newcomb enlisted in Company B, 4th Vermont Infantry Regiment, in Williamstown on August 23, 1861. Newcomb was a diminutive fellow measuring only five feet, three and a half inches tall. In 1862, he was assigned as a division teamster. He deserted on July 18, 1863, while the army was moving south after the Battle of Gettysburg. There is no record of his whereabouts after he deserted.[44]

Don P. Nichols

Company B

Don P. Nichols enlisted in Company B, 4th Vermont Infantry Regiment, in Williamstown on August 17, 1861. He was captured in the Battle of Savage Station, a few miles south of Richmond, Virginia, on June 29, 1862. He was paroled on September 13, 1862, and sent to Camp Parole in Annapolis, Maryland, to recuperate before being sent back to his regiment. He deserted at Camp Parole on September 28, 1862.[45]

Frank W. Sancry

Company B

Frank W. Sancry was born in Williamstown. He enlisted at eighteen years of age in Company B, 4th Vermont Infantry Regiment, in Williamstown on August 24, 1861. Sancry reenlisted on December 15, 1863, and received a $300 bounty from Williamstown. He was promoted to corporal on February 29, 1864, and to sergeant on September 20, 1864. Sancry was promoted to first sergeant of Company B on January 1, 1865, and was mustered out of service on July 13, 1865.[46]

Henry M. Smith

Company B

Henry M. Smith, son of Oren and Deborah Clark Smith of Williamstown, enlisted in Company B, 4th Vermont Infantry Regiment, in Williamstown on September 5, 1861. He was promoted to corporal on March 4, 1864. Smith was slightly wounded on May 20, 1864, at the Battle of Chancellorsville, Virginia. He was wounded again on June 20, 1864, in the trenches outside Petersburg, Virginia. This time he was not so lucky. He died of his wound on July 1 and was buried at City Point National Cemetery in Hopewell, Virginia. There is a cenotaph for him at Williamstown's West Hill Cemetery.[47]

William Twaddle

Company G

William Twaddle was born in Canada. He enlisted in Company G, 4th Vermont Infantry Regiment, in Williamstown on September 3, 1861. He was captured, along with 402 other Vermonters, on June 23, 1864, at the Battle of Weldon Railroad on the outskirts of Petersburg, Virginia. He died of scurvy at the Andersonville prisoner of war camp on October 26, 1864, and was buried in section H, grave no. 11476, in what is now the Andersonville National Cemetery.[48]

Daniel G. Webster

Company B

Daniel G. Webster of Williamstown married Mary E. Wise in Washington, Vermont, on April 10, 1861. She had been married before, to an Enos Wise. In the winter of 1858 or '59, Mary and Enos were living in Crown Point, New York, where Enos was found lying in the road dying by a group of schoolchildren. He was carried to a nearby house, where he died. Webster enlisted in Company B, 4th Vermont Infantry Regiment, on August 17, 1861, in Chelsea, Vermont. At the time of his enlistment, he was twenty-four years old and had blue eyes and light hair. He stood five feet, five inches tall and listed his occupation as a farmer. He contracted measles while in the army and as a result was given a disability discharge for aphonia (inability to produce speech sounds) and epileptic seizures on November 5, 1862. He received a government disability pension of eight dollars a month beginning on July 10, 1863. He apparently recovered from his illnesses, as he enlisted in Company C, 8th Vermont Infantry Regiment, on August 15, 1864 (see p. 81).[49]

Henry L. Wilson

Company B

Henry L. Wilson, son of Clark and Polly Wilson of Williamstown, enlisted in Company B, 4th Vermont Infantry Regiment, in Williamstown on August

23, 1861. He was promoted to corporal on April 1, 1863. He reenlisted on February 11, 1864, and received a $300 bounty from Williamstown. Wilson was assigned as a Sixth Corps mail carrier in July 1864, a position he kept until he finished his military service. He was promoted to sergeant on January 25, 1865. Henry Wilson was mustered out of service on July 13, 1865. After the war, he returned to Williamstown, where he died of tuberculosis on February 17, 1867, and was buried at Williamstown's Village Cemetery. Wilson never married.[50]

WILLIAM CLARK WILSON

Company B

William C. Wilson enlisted in Company B, 4th Vermont Infantry Regiment, in Williamstown on August 27, 1861. He was wounded in the left leg on December 13, 1862, at the Battle of Fredericksburg, Virginia. His leg was amputated, and he died from complications of the operation on January 7, 1863. His body was sent home, and he was buried at Williamstown's East Hill Cemetery.[51]

7

5TH VERMONT INFANTRY REGIMENT

The 5th Vermont was mustered into service on September 16, 1861, in St. Albans, Vermont, under the command of Colonel Henry A. Smalley. Within a few days, it was in Arlington, Virginia, where it joined the 2nd and 3rd Vermont. In the 5th Vermont's first major battle on June 29, 1862, at Savage Station, Virginia, the regiment suffered tremendous losses. With Colonel Smalley being ill, the regiment was under the command of its lieutenant colonel, Lewis A. Grant. Of the 400 troops that went into the fight, 45 men were killed and 143 were wounded, 27 of whom died later of their wounds. The 5th Vermont fought with the Vermont Brigade during its entire four years of service. After Colonel Smalley retired from the army in September 1862, Lieutenant Colonel Lewis A. Grant was promoted to command the regiment. Colonel Grant was promoted to brigadier general in February 1863 and given command of the Vermont Brigade. Lieutenant Colonel John R. Lewis replaced Colonel Grant in command of the 5th Vermont. The 5th Vermont was mustered out of service on June 29, 1865.[52]

James R. Martin

Company I

James R. Martin, son of L. and M. Martin of Williamstown, enlisted in Company I, 5th Vermont Infantry Regiment, in Rutland on September 4, 1861. He was wounded on July 10, 1863, at the Battle of Funkstown,

Camp of the 5th Vermont Infantry Regiment at Camp Griffin, Virginia. Photograph by George H. Houghton. *Courtesy of the Vermont Historical Society.*

Maryland. He reenlisted on December 15, 1863. He was promoted to corporal and then to sergeant on March 1, 1864. On May 6, 1864, he was wounded in the stomach in the Battle of the Wilderness. When the bullet entered, it took little bits of his uniform with it and then perforated his colon. After receiving care in field hospitals, he was admitted to the Armory Square Hospital in Washington, D.C., on May 28. On September 23, he was admitted to Sloan General Hospital, where he seemed to be improving and was given a furlough to go home to recuperate. His parents were at the time living in Northfield. Unfortunately, James took a turn for the worse and died in his parents' home on November 25, 1864.[53]

HENRY H. RECOR

Company A

Henry H. Recor, son of Max and Addle Jellie Recor, both Canadians, was born in Chazey, New York. At some point he moved to Williamstown, where he enlisted in Company D, 12th Vermont Infantry Regiment, on October 22,

1862. After serving his nine months' service, he was mustered out with his regiment on July 14, 1863. After almost a year at home, Recor was tempted by money to go back into the army. Jude Town, of Barre, paid Recor $300 to be his substitute. Recor was assigned to Company A, 5th Vermont, on June 4, 1864. Later, on January 2, 1865, he was promoted to corporal in Company A (see p. 116).

On April 1, 1865, the Army of the Potomac was formed in the dark of night in front of its fortifications for the final breakthrough at Petersburg, Virginia. The 5th Vermont was the tip of the spear for this attack, which was to take place the next day at 4:30 a.m. Captain Charles G. Gould, commander of Company H and part of Company A, was somehow placed out in front of some other Federal units, which, unable to distinguish friend from foe in the darkness, would fire on Gould and his men when the charge started. The few officers available quickly gathered and decided that their only recourse was, when the order to charge was given, to charge straight into the Rebel artillery fortification in front of them.

When the order to charge was given, Company A charged into the darkness toward the fort in front under a murderous fire. As the Vermonters neared the Rebel fortifications, they encountered abatis (downed trees facing toward the enemy with the ends of the limbs sharpened). By chance, Captain Gould found a path through the abatis and led his men through. Because the path was narrow, only a few men could get through at a time. Unaware that no one was behind him, Captain Gould jumped into the ditch in front of the fort and climbed the parapet. When Gould reached the top, he was looking into the muzzle of a Confederate musket. Fortunately, the musket misfired, and Gould immediately sank his sword into the man who was trying to shoot him, killing him. Then, as Gould jumped into the fort, a bayonet was thrust into his mouth and came out his left cheek. At almost the same time, a Rebel officer armed with a sword slashed him on the head. "The remainder of my brief stay in the work," as Gould described later, "was a confused scramble, from which, had my assailants been fewer in number, I should scarcely have escaped. As it was, firing on their part would have been dangerous for their own men; consequently their efforts were apparently restricted to the use of bayonets and clubbed muskets." During the struggle, one of the Rebels grabbed Gould's overcoat and pulled it over his head, while another stabbed him in the back between the shoulder blades with a bayonet. This was the most severe of his wounds. The bayonet entered his spine and penetrated it nearly to the spinal cord. That was about the last thing Gould remembered. The Rebels then started beating him with the butts of their muskets. That was when Corporal Henry Recor jumped into the fortification and, with "super human strength," pushed and beat the Rebels back and started dragging his company commander out of the fort. Just as they reached the top of the parapet, Recor was hit by a piece of shell fragment in the left leg.

The fragment hit him about six inches below the knee on his left leg and took out some muscle, injured the bone and cut one of the tendons, but Recor managed to drag the captain to safety. Recor was taken to the hospital at City Point, Virginia, where he stayed for a month before being sent to Mount Pleasant Hospital in Washington, D.C. After a three-month stay at Mount Pleasant Hospital, Recor was sent to Sloan General Hospital in Montpelier, from which he was discharged from the army on July 11, 1865.

Henry H. Recor was noted in the official report of the breakthrough for gallant and meritorious conduct during the attack. In fact, along with a number of other enlisted men, he was nominated by his brigade commander for the Medal of Honor, but Recor was not selected. Recor had a nice

Captain Charles G. Gould, Company H, 5th Vermont Infantry Regiment. *Courtesy of the Vermont Historical Society.*

surprise, though, when he mustered out of service on June 19, 1865. He was given a $150 cash award for his heroism at Petersburg.

In June 1865, when Recor applied for a disability pension, Captain Gould wrote an affidavit for him that stated:

> *That while in said service and in the line of his duty, at the assault upon the enemy's works at Petersburg, Va., on the 2nd day of April 1865, he performed a noble act of bravery, periling his own life to save mine, and was wounded in said battle by a piece of shell in his left leg.*

Recor's pension was approved for his leg wound, rheumatism and heart trouble, and he received a modest monthly stipend for the rest of his life.

After the war, Henry married Alvira Vasser on June 16, 1865, in Plattsburg, New York. After their marriage, they lived in Williamstown, where Henry worked as a stonemason. Over the years, Henry and Alvira had four children: Charles, born on May 15, 1866; Alice M., born on August 2, 1871; Bessie O., born on June 19, 1879; and Blanch B., born on March 30, 1882. In 1873, the Recors were living in Barre. In 1903, they moved from Barre to Manchester, New Hampshire, where Henry died of a cerebral hemorrhage on March 24. His body was brought back to Barre for burial. Alvira died on September 1, 1924.[54]

8
6TH VERMONT INFANTRY REGIMENT

The 6th Vermont, under the command of Colonel Nathan Lord Jr., of Montpelier, was mustered into service at Montpelier, Vermont, on October 19, 1861, and left the same day for Virginia. It joined the Vermont Brigade on October 24 and fought in every battle with the brigade until the end of the war. Colonel Lord resigned for health reasons on December 18, 1862, and was replaced by Oscar S. Tuttle of Cavendish. Tuttle resigned due to a serious illness on March 18, 1863, and was replaced by Swanton, Vermont native Elisha L. Barney. Colonel Barney was mortally wounded in the Battle of the Wilderness on May 5, 1864, and died on May 10. Sumner H. Lincoln replaced Barney and commanded the regiment for the rest of the war. The 6th Vermont was mustered out of service on July 8, 1865.[55]

Elmer W. Boutwell

Company B

Elmer W., the son of Samuel P. and Lydia Allen Boutwell, was born in Williamstown in 1843. When he completed his education, he worked with his father on the family farm. Boutwell enlisted in Company B, 6th Vermont Infantry Regiment, in Williamstown on October 3, 1861. When he enlisted, he was eighteen years old, stood six feet tall and had a dark complexion, dark hair and blue eyes. While at Harrison's Landing, Virginia, after the ill-fated

Peninsula Campaign, Boutwell started having fevers that eventually led to heart trouble. He was treated at Chesapeake General Hospital in Hampton, Virginia; at the Sixteenth Street Hospital in Philadelphia, Pennsylvania; at the Chestnut Hill Hospital, also in Philadelphia; and, finally, at the Convalescent Camp in Alexandria, Virginia, where he was given a disability discharge on March 27, 1863. After the war, he worked as a farmer and shoemaker and lived in Methuen, Massachusetts, and Hopkins, New Hampshire. He married Julia A. Woodbury, and they had one daughter named Lefie C. Boutwell, who was born on May 29, 1878. Elmer died of heart disease in Hopkins on April 29, 1894, and was buried there. In 1896, Julia began receiving a ten-dollar-a-month government widow's pension. Julia died on July 29, 1908.[56]

Henry H. Boutwell

Company B

Henry H. Boutwell, son of Samuel P. and Lydia Allen Boutwell, was born on April 3, 1837, in Williamstown. He enlisted in Company B, 6th Vermont Infantry Regiment, in Williamstown on October 3, 1861. He was promoted to corporal on January 10, 1862. Boutwell was given a disability discharge on August 27, 1862, for chronic diarrhea and heart trouble. After returning to Williamstown, he married Philinda Mason on October 11, 1863. After recovering from his illness he contracted in the army, Boutwell enlisted in the 3rd Vermont Light Artillery on August 29, 1864 (see p. 142).[57]

Martin Burnham

Company C

Martin Burnham married Martha Martin in Williamstown on November 2, 1853. He enlisted in Company G, 6th Vermont Infantry Regiment, in Williamstown on August 14, 1861. At the time of his enlistment, he was twenty-two years old and stood five feet, five and a half inches tall. He had blue eyes and listed his occupation as a farmer. He was wounded on June 30, 1862, at the Battle of Savage Station below Richmond, Virginia. Because the Army of the Potomac was on the retreat and being pressed by the Rebels, most of the wounded were left at Savage Station, where a field hospital had been established. These men were captured by the Rebels. Burnham was one of those unfortunate men. He was paroled three months later, on September 28, 1862. While in the hospital at Camp Parole in Annapolis, Maryland, Martin deserted. He was caught and arrested while trying to enlist in a cavalry regiment and returned to Camp Parole. A note sent with him read, "This man is a deserter from 5th Vermont Vols. Is an insolent sullen Man. Refused for a long time to give his name." For some reason, Martin was not punished for deserting and was given a disability discharge on November 1, 1862. He then enlisted in the Veteran Reserve Corps.[58]

Orange H. Dickinson

Company A

Orange H. Dickinson was born on March 11, 1846. He enlisted in Company E, 13th Vermont Infantry Regiment, in Cambridge, Vermont, on September 8, 1862. He was mustered out of service with his regiment on July 21, 1863. After returning home, Dickinson enlisted in Company A, 6th Vermont Infantry Regiment, in Cambridge on March 1, 1865, and was mustered out of service on June 26, 1865. Orange's wife, Nancy, died on April 11, 1897, and was buried at Williamstown's Village Cemetery. Orange died on December 16, 1904, and was buried beside his wife (see p. 123).[59]

Frederick G. Doyle

Company B

Frederick G. Doyle, the son of William P. and Anna Doyle, was born in Hartford, Connecticut. He enlisted in Company B, 6th Vermont Infantry Regiment, in Williamstown on October 3, 1861, at age sixteen or seventeen. What he was doing in Williamstown at the time is unknown. He was a small boy, measuring only five feet, five inches tall.

Anna married William P. Doyle in Dublin, Ireland, on June 17, 1827. The Doyles immigrated to the United States and settled in Windsor, Connecticut, on October 1, 1849. Then, sometime afterward, they moved to New Britain, Connecticut, where Anna separated from William on about

January 1, 1852, for intolerable cruelty and filed for divorce. At the time, she had four minor children: William J. Doyle, age nine; Frederick G. Doyle, age seven; Edward Doyle, age four; and Alice Doyle, age two and a half. Her divorce was final on August 13, 1852. Times were extremely tough for Anna and her children, and after the outbreak of the Civil War, Anna went to work as a nurse at the Mansion House General Hospital in Alexandria, Virginia, in December 1861.

In a letter to his mother, dated December 20, 1861, Frederick, who had enlisted two months earlier, said he would have his seven-dollar-a-month state pay sent directly to her, and he would send an additional ten dollars a month from his thirteen-dollar-a-month army pay. In writing to his brother, William, on March 13, 1863, he said, "Just think how mother has worked for us. She has slaved and toiled her life away for us and now we must do what we can for her, for my part I will freely give her every cent hereafter that I can."

During the Chancellorsville Campaign, the Sixth Corps of the Army of the Potomac was assigned the mission of taking Fredericksburg from Confederate hands, while Major General Joseph Hooker and the rest of the army fought at Chancellorsville. The Sixth Corps was successful in taking Fredericksburg on May 3, 1863, but the next day, while moving toward Chancellorsville to reinforce Hooker, the Sixth Corps was surrounded by Rebel forces on three sides near Bank's Ford. The Rebels launched several vicious attacks on the stranded Federal corps.

The last Rebel charge was directed at what seemed to be a gap in the Vermont Brigade's line. What the Confederates did not know, however, was that the commander of the 6th Vermont had his men lying down behind a small rise. The Vermont officers cautioned their men to "Hold your fire, boys!" and "Keep quiet there!" Then, when the Confederate line got to within twenty feet of the 6th Vermont, the Green Mountain Boys sprang up and gave it a volley straight into its face. The 6th Vermont's commander screamed, "Charge boys, charge!" The impromptu charge cleared the regiment's entire front of the gray-clad troops. In the process, they captured a colonel, a lieutenant colonel, a major, 17 company grade officers and 237 enlisted men. Unfortunately, in this charge Private Frederick G. Doyle was shot dead. After his death, Frederick's mother, Anna, quit her nursing position of eighteen months and went in search of her son's body. Whether she found his body is unknown.

In April 1864, Anna applied for a dependent mother's pension from the government, as it was Frederick who had supplied the majority of her support. She received approval of the eight-dollar-a-month pension on July 27, 1864, backdated to May 4, 1863, the date of Frederick's death. At the time she received the pension, she was living in New York City.[60]

GEORGE G. EDSON

Company B

George G. Edson enlisted in Company B, 6th Vermont Infantry Regiment, in Williamstown on October 3, 1861. He was given a disability discharge for disease on May 21, 1862, and returned to Williamstown. After recovering from his illness, Edson enlisted in Company G, 10th Vermont Infantry Regiment, on August 29, 1864 (see p. 93).[61]

DANIEL GRANGER

Company F

Daniel Granger was born on May 29, 1833, in Bethel, Vermont. He enlisted in Company F, 6th Vermont Infantry Regiment, in Williamstown on September 21, 1861. He died of typhoid fever on January 12, 1862, in the regimental hospital at Camp Griffin, in Arlington, Virginia. His personal effects were sold, and the money was sent to his wife. He has a stone at Williamstown's Village Cemetery, but it is unknown whether his body was sent home for burial or the stone is a cenotaph.[62]

HENRY H. MARSH

Company B

Henry H. Marsh was born in Williamstown. He enlisted in Company B, 6th Vermont Infantry Regiment, in Williamstown on September 30, 1861, at age twenty. He was wounded in the leg and taken prisoner at Fredericksburg, Virginia, on May 3, 1863. Marsh was paroled on May 16, 1863. He died of his wounds in the Armory Street Hospital in Washington, D.C., on August 22, 1863, and was buried at the Soldier's Home National

Cemetery in Washington, D.C. Marsh's personal effects were sent home to his parents. They consisted of one tobacco pouch, two portfolios, one pocketbook, one gold pen with its case, thirty-five cents in change and one likeness (photograph).[63]

Henry Martin

Company G

Henry Martin, son of Allen and Betsy Martin, was born in Barre, Vermont, on June 7, 1829. He married Lestina Phelps, daughter of C.C. and Lorinda Phelps of Barre, before the war. They had two sons, Sidney I. and Clayton H. Martin. Henry enlisted in Company G, 6th Vermont Infantry Regiment, in Williamstown on August 18, 1863, as a paid substitute for Benjamin O. Flint of Williamstown. Flint had to pay Martin a sum of $300 to go into the army for him. At the age of thirty-four, Henry Martin was much older than most other privates in the army. Probably because of his education and maturity, Martin quickly rose through the ranks. He was promoted to corporal on September 23, 1864, and to sergeant on June 20, 1865. On June 23, 1865, he was promoted to adjutant of his regiment, but he only held that rank for three days before being mustered out of service on June 26. Sometime after leaving the army, Henry Martin purchased a farm in Williamstown, where he spent the rest of his life raising produce.

Henry Martin, Company G, 6th Vermont Infantry Regiment. *Courtesy of the U.S. Army Military History Institute.*

Lestina Martin died of an inward rupture on September 8, 1868, at age thirty-one and was buried at Williamstown's

Village Cemetery. Henry next married Lois N. Bond, daughter of Stephen B. Bond of Topsham, Vermont, and they had one child, a son whom they named Allen. Henry Martin was a prosperous farmer and a very civic-minded man. He served as a selectman and lister, as well as a state legislator. Henry had a close call on Friday evening, September 19, 1890. While he and Wilber F. Levings were crossing the bridge below the residence of M.A. Smith, their horse ran off the lower side of the bridge, and horse, carriage and passengers fell about ten feet to the rocks below. Help soon came, and the horse and the wagon were taken back to the road without any serious injury or damage. Martin and Levings escaped with only a few severe bruises. Henry Martin died of heart disease at age seventy-one on July 11, 1900, and was buried at Williamstown's Village Cemetery. Lois Martin died of heart problems on November 25, 1929, in Essex, Vermont, and was buried at Williamstown's Village Cemetery with her husband.[64]

CORNELIUS MCMULLEN

Company B

Cornelius McMullen was born in Williamstown on December 22, 1833. He enlisted in Company B, 6th Vermont Infantry Regiment, in Williamstown on October 3, 1861. McMullen was promoted to corporal on November 25, 1861. He was later reduced to private for some unrecorded reason. Cornelius reenlisted on December 15, 1863, and mustered out of service on June 26, 1865. After the war, Cornelius returned to Vermont, where he married Eliza J. Maxwell in 1865. Eliza died in 1892. Cornelius died in 1895 and was buried beside his wife at Irasville Cemetery in Waitsfield, Vermont.[65]

JOHN O'RILEY

Company B

John O'Riley enlisted in Williamstown in Company B, 6th Vermont Infantry Regiment, on October 3, 1861. He was given a disability discharge for illness on February 22, 1864, for some unspecified disease. John married a woman named Maria in Chicago, Illinois, on May 18, 1869. After he died, Maria applied for, but did not receive, a pension. At the time, she lived in Vershire, Vermont.[66]

William Raycroft

Company B and Company K

William Raycroft was born in County Cork, Ireland, on January 21, 1840. He enlisted in Company B, 6th Vermont Infantry Regiment, in Williamstown on September 29, 1861. Raycroft was promoted to corporal on December 6, 1862, and later to sergeant. He was wounded on May 3, 1863, at the Second Battle of Fredericksburg. Raycroft reenlisted on December 15, 1863, and received a $300 bounty from Williamstown. He was wounded again on May 5, 1864, at the Battle of the Wilderness. He was promoted to second lieutenant in Company K of the 6th Vermont on November 12, 1864. Raycroft was wounded for a third time on October 19, 1864, at the Battle of Cedar Creek, Virginia. He was promoted to first lieutenant in Company K on April 22, 1865. William Raycroft was

Postwar photograph of William Raycroft, Company K, 6th Vermont Infantry Regiment. *Courtesy of the Vermont Historical Society.*

mustered out of service on June 26, 1865. He married Eliza Kelty, and they had a farm near what is now McDonald Road in Williamstown. William died of a pulmonary hemorrhage on July 28, 1903, and was buried at St. Johns Cemetery in Northfield, Vermont. One of his children, Joseph Raycroft, born in Williamstown on November 15, 1867, became a doctor and was known at Princeton University as the father of intramural sports. He developed physical fitness training for the U.S. Army in World War I and for the U.S. Navy in World War II.[67]

ELIJAH J. WILLIAMS

Company D

Elijah J. Williams was born in Williamstown. He enlisted in Company D, 6th Vermont Infantry Regiment, in Barton, Vermont, on August 11, 1864, at age forty-one. He was promoted to corporal on February 2, 1864. Williams was wounded in the thigh in the Battle of the Wilderness on May 5, 1864, and died of his wound on May 9. He has a cenotaph in Williamstown's West Hill Cemetery. He had been married to Pamela S. Williams, and she died on March 23, 1859.[68]

9

7th Vermont Infantry Regiment

The 7th Vermont Infantry Regiment was mustered into service on February 12, 1862, in Rutland, Vermont. It, along with the 8th Vermont, was designated to be part of a division being formed by Major General Benjamin F. Butler, whose mission was to capture New Orleans. The 7th Vermont left Rutland on March 10 and arrived at Ship Island, south of New Orleans, on April 7. New Orleans was successfully captured on April 25, 1862. The 7th Vermont remained in the Deep South for the rest of the war and participated in the Siege of Vicksburg, the Battle of Baton Rouge and the Mobile Campaign, as well as a number of skirmishes.

The 7th Vermont had the dubious distinction of being the longest-serving Vermont regiment. On June 2, 1865, the Vermonters sailed to Brazos, Texas, where they joined the Army of Observation under Major General Godfrey Weitzel. Weitzel's mission was to await the outcome of France's attempt to establish an empire in Mexico. France's attempt, however, was unsuccessful, and the 7th Vermont was mustered out of service on March 14, 1866.[69]

Nathan B. Capron

Company G

Nathan B. Capron, son of Ephriam Capron, was born in Williamstown on June 20, 1818. He married Betsey E. Eaton in Walden, Vermont, on May 3, 1839. At age forty-four, he enlisted in Company G, 7th Vermont

Infantry Regiment, in Williamstown on May 26, 1862. Capron stood five feet, eight and a half inches tall. He had a light complexion, blue eyes and light hair and listed his occupation as a carpenter. June 1863 found the 7th Vermont at Fort Barrancas, Florida. Here, many of the men were detailed to reinforce the fortifications, and in doing so, Capron got a hernia. He was sent to the regimental surgeon and finally to the Marine General Hospital, New Orleans. Capron was given a disability discharge from the Marine Hospital on March 28, 1865. Not long after returning home, Capron moved to Danville, Vermont, sometime about 1868. In 1888, he lived in Providence, Rhode Island, where he died on July 9 and was buried at the North Burial Grounds.[70]

PETER DUCLOW

Company K

Peter Duclow was born on April 10, 1826, in St. Matthews, Canada. Exactly when he moved to Williamstown is not known, but he appears as a Williamstown resident in the 1860 U.S. census. He enlisted in Company A, 1st Vermont Infantry Regiment, in Northfield on May 2, 1861. Duclow served his three months with the regiment and was mustered out of service on August 15, 1861. After leaving the army, he returned home and married Martha Deyatte in Northfield on September 1, 1861. Duclow enlisted in Company K, 7th Vermont Infantry Regiment, in Williamstown on January 2, 1862. At that time, he was twenty-two years old. He stood five feet, five and a half inches tall and had a light complexion, blue eyes and dark hair. He listed his occupation as a farm laborer. He was promoted to corporal on March 1, 1863. He was mustered out of service on September 27, 1864, by special order of the War Department because of chronic diarrhea. After his discharge, he and Martha returned to Canada. Then, they moved to Connecticut. After a while, they moved to North Stanbridge, Canada. As he grew older, Peter suffered from piles, rheumatism, bad eyes and heart disease. By age seventy-two, he was so infirm that he was permanently stooped over and was receiving a twenty-dollar-a-month government pension.[71]

James F. Randall

Company K

James F. Randall enlisted in Company F, 1st Vermont Infantry Regiment, in Berlin, Vermont, on May 2, 1861, and was mustered out of service with his regiment on August 15, 1861. He enlisted in Company C, 1st Vermont Cavalry Regiment, in Berlin on September 19, 1861. Because of his previous service, Randall was selected as a corporal. He was discharged for a disability in January 1862. After recovering from his illness, he enlisted in Company K, 7th Vermont Infantry Regiment, in Williamstown on August 28, 1864, and received a $600 town bounty. Randall was wounded on March 31, 1865, at the Battle of Mobile, Alabama, and was mustered out of service on August 7, 1865. After the war, Randall lived in Montpelier and worked as a house painter and paperhanger. He died on October 28, 1903, at age sixty-seven of heart trouble after a long illness. He was buried at the Cutler Cemetery in East Montpelier on November 7 and left no children.[72]

10

8TH VERMONT INFANTRY REGIMENT

The 8th Vermont Infantry Regiment was mustered into service in Brattleboro on February 18, 1862. On April 6, the regiment arrived at Ship Island, just south of New Orleans, where it joined the 7th Vermont and Major General Benjamin F. Butler's Division. After the capture of New Orleans on April 24, the 8th Vermont went on to participate in the Port Hudson Campaign, as well as a number of small battles and skirmishes in the Deep South. On June 19, 1864, the 8th Vermont was ordered north to join the Army of the Potomac in Virginia. The Vermonters reached Washington, D.C., on July 13 and immediately joined Federal forces in pursuing Lieutenant General Jubal A. Early's army, which had just days before threatened Washington. Within days, the 8th Vermont was assigned to Major General Philip H. Sheridan's Army of the Shenandoah and spent the rest of the summer and fall in the Shenandoah Valley. During that time it fought in the Battles of Opequon, Fisher's Hill, Cedar Creek and Newtown. The 8th Vermont's toughest fight was at Cedar Creek, where it went into battle with just over two hundred men and had fifteen men killed, eighty-two wounded and twenty-seven missing. The 8th Vermont was mustered out of service on June 21, 1865.[73]

John W. Bacon

Company E

John W. Bacon enlisted in Company E, 3rd Vermont Infantry Regiment, in Williamstown on November 12, 1861. He received a disability discharge on October 31, 1862. After recovering from his injuries, Bacon enlisted in Company E, 8th Vermont Infantry Regiment, on September 17, 1864, in Williamstown and received a $600 town bounty. Without receiving another scratch, he was mustered out of the army on June 1, 1865. After his discharge from the army, Bacon returned to Williamstown and went back to farming. He also received a $4-a-month government disability pension. As the years went by, he suffered more and more from the injury. In March 1901, his doctor, George B. Nichols of Barre, stated that Bacon had

> *a good deal of trouble about passing his urine from the bladder owing* [to] *a crushing injury received in the army. He passes it from four to fifteen times a day, and nights as often as twelve times. I was called one time to see him, when I was unable to pass a catheter. There seems to be a cul-de-sac into which the catheter passes instead into the bladder. He has a good deal of pain in the region of the middle lumbar vertebrae with a sense of coldness at that point.*

John Bacon died of ascites (a collection of fluid in the abdomen), kidney failure and heart disease on August 9, 1908, at age seventy-two in Williamstown. Both the ascites and the kidney failure were results of his injury while in the army. He was buried at East Hill Cemetery on August 11, 1908. After his death, his wife, Sarah, received a twelve-dollar-a-month government widow's pension starting on September 8, 1908. Sarah died in the home of Frank Ashline at 54 South Main Street in Barre on March 27, 1909, and was buried at Williamstown's Village Cemetery (see p. 30).[74]

James H. Bailey

Company K

James H. Bailey, son of George H. and Reland Bailey, married Persis P. Abbott on July 25, 1860, in Williamstown. At age twenty-eight, he enlisted in Company K, 8th Vermont Infantry Regiment, in Williamstown on

December 29, 1863. Although he listed his occupation as a physician, Bailey served in the ranks as a private. For his service, he received a $315 bounty from the town. For a while, he was assigned as a clerk at Nineteenth Corps headquarters. He was mustered out of service on March 10, 1864, due to illness. What happened to James H. Bailey after the war remains a mystery.[75]

JAMES BASS

Company C

James Bass, son of James M. and Alma Poole Bass, was born in Williamstown on April 12, 1846. He enlisted in Company C, 8th Vermont Infantry Regiment, on December 26, 1863, and received a $315 town bounty. He was mustered out of service on June 28, 1865. After the war, James Bass moved west.[76]

FABER BENEDICT

Company C

Faber Benedict, son of Martin M. and Althea Coleman Benedict, was born on November 12, 1845, in Malone, New York. He enlisted in Company C, 8th Vermont Infantry Regiment, in Williamstown on August 23, 1864, at age nineteen and received a $600 town bounty. The constant marching caused varicose veins in Benedict's right leg. After the Battle of Cedar Creek in the fall of 1864, Benedict's right leg ached so bad that his tent mates—George Bruce, George D. Marston and William Foster—would rub his leg so he could go to sleep. Faber was mustered out of the army on June 1, 1865, at the expiration of his service. After the war, Faber Benedict married Mary Asenith Davenport on February 16, 1867, in East Roxbury, Vermont. They lived in Williamstown for a while and then moved to Bethel, Vermont. Faber and Mary had four children: Willard E., born on March 6, 1868; Burton H., born on October 29, 1872; Clyde E., born on April 29, 1878; and Leslie O., born on March 21, 1881. Later in life, he received a small government disability pension for his varicose veins and rheumatism. Faber Benedict died of heart disease in Randolph Center, Vermont, on December 8, 1920, and was buried at East Bethel Cemetery.[77]

George W. Blanchard

Company E

George W. Blanchard, son of Hiram and Parthenia Mary Earle Blanchard, was born in Barre, Vermont. He enlisted in Company I, 13th Vermont Infantry Regiment, in Barre on September 7, 1861, and was mustered out on July 21, 1863. Blanchard returned to Barre, where he enlisted in Company E, 8th Vermont Infantry Regiment, on December 3, 1863. Most of his time in the 8th Vermont was spent in the regimental band. He mustered out on June 28, 1865. When he returned from the war, George and his brother, Origen A. Blanchard, who served in Company D, 2nd Vermont, bought a farm together in Williamstown, where they spent the rest of their lives. During the winters, George taught music (see p. 122).[78]

George Edger Bruce

Company C

George E. Bruce was born in Peterborough, New Hampshire. He enlisted in Company C, 8th Vermont Infantry Regiment, in Williamstown on August 18, 1864. He was a tall lad, measuring five feet, eleven inches tall. He listed his occupation as a shoemaker. He told the recruiting officer that he was twenty-two years old, but in fact he was only seventeen, having been born on July 18, 1847. While in winter camp in Petersburg, Virginia, George was in a detail chopping down trees for firewood. Someone behind him downed a tree, and one of the branches struck George on his back and left shoulder. During the Grand Review in Washington, D.C., in June 1865, George was troubled with heart problems. Both of these ailments would plague him for the rest of his life. He was mustered out on June 28, 1865. After the war, George Bruce, at age fifty-two, married Sarah Seaver, daughter of Ansil and Clarissa Seaver, in Williamstown. They had two children: Frank, born on May 13, 1868, and Nettie, born on March 1870. Sometime in early 1870, Sarah died. On April 1, 1875, George married Malona R. Hanks in Warren, Vermont. After they were married, George and Sarah resided in Warren, where he was a member of the Joseph Eldridge Post, No. 36, of the Grand Army of the Republic. As time went by, George suffered more and more from the injuries he received in the army and was awarded a government disability pension. He died of diabetes on May 2, 1902, and was buried at Warren's Village Cemetery. Sarah died on January 29, 1904.[79]

JUDSON CLOUGH

Company C

Judson Clough enlisted in Company C, 8th Vermont Infantry Regiment, in Williamstown on November 19, 1861, at age twenty-four. He was mustered out at the expiration of his service on June 22, 1864. Nothing is known of Clough after he was mustered out of the army.[80]

HENRY A. DOW

Company C

Henry A. Dow was born in Peacham, Vermont, on February 19, 1843. He enlisted in Company I, 13th Vermont Infantry Regiment, in Barre, Vermont, on August 25, 1862. He mustered out with his regiment on July 21, 1863. On December 26, 1863, six months after returning home, Dow enlisted in Company C, 8th Vermont Infantry Regiment, in Williamstown and received a $315 town bounty. He was wounded in the right hand by a Minié ball on September 19, 1864, at the Battle of Winchester, Virginia. The bullet mangled his third and fourth fingers, causing them to be permanently contracted. He was mustered out on June 1, 1864. A year after he returned from the army, on October 2, 1865, Dow married Isabella A. Luce in Plainfield, Vermont. According to the U.S. census of 1880, Dow and his wife were living in Marshfield, Vermont. By February 19, 1918, he was getting a $30-a-month government pension for his war wound. In 1920, Henry and Isabella were living in Cabot, Vermont, where he died of influenza on March 10, 1932. He was buried at Cabot's Village Cemetery. His son applied for and received a burial flag from the Veterans Administration for his father's funeral (see p. 123).[81]

Horace S. Farnham

Company C

Horace S. Farnham, son of Aaron and Lydia Seaver Farnham of Williamstown, married Abbie S. Pope, of Brookfield, on March 4, 1862. She was the daughter of Edmund and Roxana Pope and was born in Brookfield. Abbie died two months after her marriage on May 9, 1862. Horace enlisted in Company D, 12th Vermont Infantry Regiment, in Williamstown on August 22, 1862, at age thirty-three. He was mustered out of service with his regiment on July 14, 1863. After returning to Williamstown, Farnham enlisted in Company C, 8th Vermont Infantry Regiment, in Williamstown on December 22, 1863, for which he received a $315 bounty from the town. He was admitted to Patterson General Hospital in Baltimore, Maryland, on August 19, 1864, and then moved to the hospital at Camp Parole in Annapolis, where he died of chronic diarrhea on September 16, 1864. Farnham was buried at Camp Parole but was later reinterred at Arlington National Cemetery (see p. 109).[82]

George R. Grant and Julius P. Kellogg

Company E

George R. Grant and his stepbrother, Julius P. Kellogg, enlisted in Company E, 8th Vermont Infantry Regiment, in Williamstown. Julius enlisted on September 6, and George enlisted two days later. There were two reasons the boys enlisted in the same regiment. First, their father had served in Company E of the 8th Vermont before dying of disease. Second, Williamstown was offering a $600 bounty, a better deal than they could get across the hill in their hometown of Northfield.

George R. Grant, son of Joseph and Mary Coburn Grant, was born in Northfield, Vermont. When he enlisted, he was eighteen years old, stood five feet, four inches tall, had blue eyes and red hair and listed his occupation as a farmer. Julius P. Kellogg, son of Truman Perrin and Alice C. Rich Kellogg, was born in Northfield on October 18, 1846.

The two boys joined their regiment while it was participating in the Shenandoah Valley Campaign in Virginia. Several days after arriving, Major General Philip H. Sheridan's army received a devastating surprise attack, just before daybreak, on October 19, by Confederate lieutenant general Jubal A. Early's forces. The Confederates had almost won the day when General Sheridan returned from Washington, D.C., just in time to rally his troops and defeat the Rebels.

During the battle, both George Grant and Julius Kellogg were wounded. Grant received a flesh wound in the left thigh. After spending almost three months in the hospital, he returned to duty on January 19, 1865. Kellogg was not as lucky as his stepbrother. He was hit by a Minié ball that passed through both of his thighs. He remained in the hospital for the rest of his time in the army, until he received a disability discharge on June 14, 1865. Because of the injury to the ligaments in his legs, he walked with most of his weight on his toes after his wound healed. He received a government disability pension for his wound.

Three months after returning to his regiment, Grant was admitted to the hospital in Winchester, Virginia, on April 30, 1865, for chronic diarrhea. Sometime later, he was evacuated back to Sloan General Hospital in Montpelier. In late June, the 8th Vermont was ordered to leave Washington, D.C., and report to Brattleboro to be mustered out of service. George Grant received orders at the hospital to join his regiment in Brattleboro to be mustered out with his comrades. On June 27, he boarded a train in Montpelier bound for Brattleboro. While the train was chugging along near Putney, Vermont, it jumped the tracks and rolled down an embankment into the Connecticut River, and Grant was killed. His body was taken to the Smith General Hospital in Brattleboro for burial. Several days after the burial, several of Grant's friends arrived in Brattleboro, had his body exhumed and took it home to Northfield, where he was buried at the Northfield Falls Cemetery.

George Grant's mother, Mary Coburn, daughter of Noel and Alice Coburn, was born in Berlin, Vermont, on May 5, 1821. Her first husband was Joseph Grant, with whom she had George R. Grant. Joseph deserted his family, and Mary divorced him. On August 20, 1859, Mary married Truman Perrin Kellogg of Worcester, Vermont. The wedding was held in Northfield, where both of them were living at the time. They had a daughter, Edith G., born on January 16, 1860, six months after they were married. Truman Kellogg's first wife, Alice, was Mary Grant's niece.

Truman Perrin Kellogg was born on February 1, 1823, in Worcester, Vermont. He had previously been married to Alice C. Rich, who died on February 25, 1859, in Worcester. Truman was commissioned as a second lieutenant in Company E, 8th Vermont Infantry Regiment, in Worcester, Vermont, on January 1, 1862. The 8th Vermont was sent to the Deep

South, where Truman Kellogg died at age thirty-eight of typhoid fever in Algiers, Louisiana, on July 23, 1862. He was initially buried in Cypress Grove, Louisiana, and then was reinterred at Chalmette National Cemetery, in Chalmette, Louisiana, near New Orleans, in section 56, grave 4424, on July 23, 1863.

Truman Kellogg, Company E, 8th Vermont Infantry Regiment. *Courtesy of the Vermont Historical Society.*

George Grant's mother, Mary Kellogg, applied for and received a twelve-dollar-a-month government widow's pension after the death of her husband, Truman. On July 9, 1872, Mary Kellogg married Azro L. Smalley in Northfield, Vermont. Azro L. Smalley, son of Jason and Margaret Smalley, was born on May 15, 1815, in Duxbury, Vermont. Mary Coburn Grant Kellogg Smalley died on May 7, 1895.

After the war, Julius P. Kellogg became a professor of mathematics at the University of Chicago. He married Hattie M. Champaign on May 7, 1874, in Detroit, Michigan. They had seven children: Aurelis C., born on February 16, 1875; Lewis M., born on November 7, 1877; Alice M., born on March 27, 1879; Clara C., born on January 24, 1883; Archel H., born on April 2, 1888; Hattie L., born on April 26, 1893; and Emma, born on March 24, 1895. Julius died of influenza and pneumonia on December 23, 1928, in Royal Oak, Michigan. He was buried in Detroit. Hattie died in September 1924 and was buried in Highland Park, Michigan.[83]

Charles Jason Green

Company C

Charles J. Green was born in Lincoln, Vermont, on February 17, 1836. He married Mary Cram, of Williamstown, on December 9, 1862. She was born on December 9, 1838. They had one child, Florence, who was born on

March 22, 1864. Mary died from complications of childbirth on April 6, 1864. Charles enlisted in Company C, 8th Vermont Infantry Regiment, in Williamstown on December 23, 1863, and received a $315 town bounty. He was transferred to the Veteran Reserve Corps on June 22, 1864, and was mustered out of service on July 18, 1865. Charles died on October 23, 1896, and was buried at the Maple Cemetery in Lincoln.[84]

WILLIAM P. HILLS

Company E

William P. Hills was born on August 7, 1844, in Duxbury, Vermont. He enlisted in Company E, 8th Vermont Infantry Regiment, in Williamstown on February 7, 1862, at age eighteen. He was promoted to corporal on February 15, 1864, and mustered out of service on June 25, 1864. He died on August 12, 1920, and was buried at the village cemetery in Waterbury, Vermont.[85]

CYRUS URBANE LATHROP

Company C

Postwar photograph of Cyrus U. Lathrop, Company C, 8th Vermont Infantry Regiment. *From* Men of Vermont.

Cyrus U. Lathrop, son of Urbane and Eliza Wiggin Lathrop, was born on October 31, 1839, in Chelsea, Vermont. In 1861, at the age of twenty-two, he bought a farm in Williamstown and married Frances A. Hopkins, daughter of Dennison and Eliza Luce Hopkins of Williamstown. They had one son, Frank D. Lathrop. Cyrus enlisted in Company C, 8th Vermont Infantry Regiment, in Williamstown on December 19, 1863, and received a $315 town bounty. He was promoted to corporal on March 30, 1865, and was mustered out of service with his regiment on June 28, 1865, without receiving a scratch in combat. After his service in the army, Cyrus returned to Williamstown and went back to farming. In 1891, he sold his farm and moved to the village, where he was involved in the sale of lumber, building materials and carriages. In 1896, he built a warehouse near the depot. He was one of the pioneers in the Williamstown Granite Co., chairman of the board of railroad commissioners for the town of Williamstown and chairman of the Williamstown Construction Co. For four years, he was associate judge of the Orange County Court, and in 1892 he was elected to represent Williamstown in the legislature. He was a charter member and commander of the William Wells GAR Post No. 113. He died of heart disease on April 14, 1908, and was buried at Williamstown's Village Cemetery. Frances died of cancer of the bowels and liver on February 28, 1925, at age eighty-two and was buried beside her husband.[86]

Isaiah Clement Little

Company E

Isaiah C. Little, the only son of Isaiah and Sally Smith Little, was born in Williamstown on June 5, 1824. He first married Martha Morrison, who died without bearing any children. He then spent three years during the gold rush near San Francisco, where he was moderately successful. After returning to Williamstown, he married Harriet Newell Corliss, of Corinth, on January 17, 1854. Little enlisted as a private in Company E, 8th Vermont Infantry Regiment, in Williamstown on December 29, 1863, and received a $315 town bounty. He served in that unit until he was mustered out of service on June 1, 1865. After his military service, Little returned to farming and raising prizewinning horses with his son, Freemont C. Little. Isaiah C. Little died on November 12, 1898, and was buried at Elmwood Cemetery in Barre, leaving behind twenty-two grandchildren.[87]

George Davenport Marston

Company C

George D. Marston, son of Asa and Hannah Davenport Marston, was born in Williamston on July 24, 1835. He married Emily Foster of Waitsfield,

Vermont, on June 28, 1863. On December 19, 1863, Marston enlisted in Company C, 8th Vermont Infantry Regiment, in Williamstown and received a $315 town bounty. He was mustered out of service on June 28, 1865. After the war, George Marston returned to Williamstown and saw his son for the first time. The son, Leslie William (Willie) Marston, was born on July 7, 1864, while George was in the army. George and Emily had two other children: Alice A., born on November 9, 1866, and Alma J., born on December 30, 1869. Alma died on December 9, 1904, and was buried at the village cemetery in Warren, Vermont. After the war, George applied for and received a $6-a-month government disability pension. In 1886, his pension was raised to $8 a month. Willie Marston died on June 29, 1952, in Northfield, Minnesota.[88]

CARLOS H. MARTIN

Company C

Carlos H. Martin, son of Dennison and Gratia H. Smith Martin, enlisted in Company D, 12th Vermont Infantry Regiment, in Williamstown on August 22, 1862. He was mustered out of service on July 14, 1863, and returned to Williamstown, but on December 30, 1863, he enlisted in Company C, 8th Vermont Infantry Regiment, for which he received a $315 bounty from the town. He was promoted to corporal on January 1, 1865. Carlos was mustered out of service on June 28, 1865, and died in 1880. His father, Dennison, died of paralysis on February 12, 1888. After her husband's death, Gratia H.S. Martin applied for a dependent mother's government pension, which was approved on May 7, 1898, for $12 a month. Gratia Martin died of heart problems on June 2, 1909, at age eighty-seven and was buried at Williamstown's Village Cemetery (see p. 115).[89]

FRANCIS (FRANK) MIZER

Company C

Frank Mizer enlisted in Company C, 8th Vermont Infantry Regiment, in Williamstown on December 26, 1863, and received a $315 town bounty. He was mustered out of service on June 28, 1865. Frank married a woman named Ellen (her maiden name is missing from his records) on July 29, 1866. They had two children: Delma, born on June 24, 1867, and Mabel, born on April 28, 1880. Frank died on March 16, 1909, in Springfield, Massachusetts.[90]

Charles E. Peters

Company D

Charles E. Peters, son of William and Mary Johnson Peters, was born in Boston on August 24, 1834. He married Lucinda Hodson, of Corinth, Vermont, on August 24, 1855, and they had two children: Charles H. and Lillian M. Peters enlisted in Company D, 1st Vermont Infantry Regiment, on May 2, 1861. At the time, he was living in Manchester, New Hampshire. He was mustered out on August 15, 1861. He enlisted in Company D, 8th Vermont Infantry Regiment, in Bradford, Vermont, on January 29, 1862. Soon after enlisting, he was detailed as assistant veterinary surgeon and later was promoted to veterinary surgeon, in which position he served until discharged for a disability on July 28, 1862. After the war, Peters worked in the livery and stage business and was also a dealer in horses in Williamstown. He died in 1903 and was buried at Lakeside Cemetery in Burlington, Vermont (see p. 15).[91]

Benjamin F. Scribner

Company C

Before the Civil War, Benjamin F. Scribner lived in Worcester, Massachusetts, where he married Abby Flagg. They had three children: William F., born on February 10, 1851; Herbert W., born on December 25, 1854; and Henry L., born on February 9, 1857. Scribner enlisted in Company C, 8th Vermont Infantry Regiment, in Williamstown on September 3, 1864, and received a $600 town bounty. Why Scribner was in Williamstown is unknown. He was mustered out of service on June 1, 1865. After the war, he received a small government disability pension for a hernia and heart disease. He lived the rest of his life in Worcester, where he worked in a shoe factory. He died on December 16, 1907.[92]

ORRIN SIMONS

Company C

Orrin Simons, the son of Martin and Orazina Carleton Simons, was born in Williamstown on May 11, 1842. He enlisted in Company D, 12th Vermont Infantry Regiment, in Williamstown on August 22, 1862. Simons was mustered out of service with his regiment on July 14, 1863. After returning home, he enlisted again on December 22, 1863, in Company C, 8th Vermont Infantry Regiment, and received a $315 town bounty. He was promoted to corporal on June 1, 1864. Simons was slightly wounded on his wrist at the Battle of Cedar Creek, Virginia, on October 19, 1864, for which he later received a small government disability pension. He was mustered out on June 28, 1865. On January 3, 1887, Orrin married Mary Beckett in Washington, D.C. She was the daughter of William S. and Polly Poole Beckett of Williamstown. One of her brothers was Andrew W. Beckett, who served in the 113th Illinois Infantry Regiment. After marrying Mary Beckett, the Simonses moved west. The couple lived for three years in Nebraska, eight years in Cheyenne, Wyoming, and then nine years in Waco, Texas. It was in Texas that Mary left Orrin, stating, "I left my husband, Orrin Simons, on the 3rd day of November, 1900. The cause of my leaving was his habitual drunkenness and inability to support me. He was so violent at times that I was afraid to remain with him." After their separation, Mary lived for some time with relatives in Washington, D.C., and later with relatives in Washington, Iowa. After Mary left, Orrin moved to Barre, Vermont. They had no children. Orrin Simons died of peritonitis in Washington, Vermont, on November 4, 1909, and was buried at Williamstown's West Hill Cemetery (see p. 120).[93]

GEORGE W. SMITH

Company G

George W. Smith was born in Middlebury, Vermont, in April 1826. He married Martha J. Bliss, and they had a son, George W. Smith Jr., born on November 13, 1861, in Wolcott, Vermont. George enlisted in Company G, 8th Vermont Infantry Regiment, in Williamstown on September 26, 1863, and received a $315 town bounty. He died of chronic diarrhea in Thibodeaux, Louisiana, on May 30, 1864, and was buried at what is now Chalmette National Cemetery in Chalmette, Louisiana, near New Orleans.[94]

Willard G. Smith

Company C

Willard G. Smith enlisted in Company C, 8th Vermont Infantry Regiment, in Williamstown on December 29, 1863, and received a $315 town bounty. He was a tall man, measuring six feet, one inch tall. He was twenty-six years old and a farmer. Smith was mustered out of service on June 28, 1865. In 1905, Willard was living in Burlington and repairing sewing machines in people's homes.[95]

Charles Clifton Staples

Company E

Charles C. Staples, son of Joseph and Emily Smalley Staples, was born in Williamstown on August 2, 1840. He enlisted in Company E, 8th Vermont Infantry Regiment, in Williamstown on December 4, 1861. He was promoted to corporal on November 1, 1864. He reenlisted on January 5, 1864, and received a $300 bounty from Williamstown. He was mustered out of service on June 28, 1865. Charles married Mary J. Dwinell

Charles C. and Mary Staples. Charles served in Company E, 8th Vermont Infantry Regiment. *Courtesy of the Williamstown Historical Society.*

in Williamstown on May 9, 1864, while he was home on reenlistment furlough. Mary was eighteen years old, and Charles was twenty-four. They had six children: Emma, born on January 12, 1868; Henry, born on March 19, 1870; Josie B., born on November 2, 1874; Dean H., born on March 14, 1878; Don, born on December 9, 1882; and Archie, born on March 22, 1888. Charles died of heart disease on December 20, 1909, and was buried at Williamstown's Village Cemetery. Mary died of nephritis on March 18, 1925, and was buried beside her husband.[96]

FRANCIS H. STAPLES

Company E

Francis H. Staples, son of Isaac S. and Rhoda Dickinson Staples, was born in Williamstown in November 1841. He married Orthelia A. Rood, daughter of Solomon and Abigail Rood of Northfield, in Williamstown on February 10, 1861. Francis enlisted in Company E, 8th Vermont Infantry Regiment, in Williamstown on January 6, 1862. On January 5, 1864, he reenlisted and received a $300 bounty from Williamstown. He was a good soldier and was rewarded by being promoted to corporal on June 8, 1864, and then to sergeant on August 23, 1864. Staples was captured on October 19, 1864, at the Battle of Cedar Creek, Virginia, and was taken to Pemberton Prison in Richmond, where he remained for a month. Next, he was sent to the prisoner of war camp in Salisbury, North Carolina, where he arrived on November 4. Here the men received terrible treatment. According to Staples, they only received one pint of cornmeal a day to eat, and it was ground with the cobs, and they had no blankets for sleeping. He watched as men from his regiment who were captured with him died one by one. The last man, Oscar Maxham, the 8th Vermont's Company E teamster, died on February 12, 1865. Suffering from scurvy, chronic diarrhea and covered with lice, Staples knew he was going to die if he did not escape. He figured his best chance of escape was to join the Confederate army, which he did. Not long after enlisting, he was sent to a camp about six miles from Salisbury, where he escaped. He was soon captured and returned to camp.

As punishment, Staples was tied up by the thumbs for one hour and then was bucked and gagged for two hours a day. This punishment lasted for ten continuous days. Both methods of punishment were common in the Civil War. Being tied by the thumbs meant being suspended by the thumbs from a limb or a pole in such a manner as to permit only one's toes to touch the ground. After an hour or more, the victim suffered extreme pain. Bucking consisted of setting the victim down, tying his wrists together, slipping them over his knees and then running a musket, or stick, beneath the knees and over the arms. Gagging involved tying a bayonet in a man's mouth. During this punishment, one of Staples's thumbs was pulled out of joint, and he lost several teeth, already loose from scurvy, from biting down on the bayonet.

After his punishment, Staples was sent with a group of men to guard a railroad bridge. The Confederates finally decided they could not trust Staples and sent him back to the prisoner of war camp in Salisbury. Back in camp, Staples and another man were sent outside the stockade, under guard, to get water. Fortunately, the guard was a loyal Union man named Lovell who had been drafted into the Confederate army. After getting away from the stockade, Lovell had the two men hide and then fired his rifle to alert the guards. When the guards arrived, Lovell sent them in the wrong direction after the two escapees. The two soldiers stayed hidden for three days. Then, they started out to find the Union lines. After fourteen days, they found the Union army Sixth Corps between Danville and Richmond, Virginia. The two former prisoners were then sent to the hospital at City Point near Petersburg. Francis Staples was honorably discharged from the army on June 28, 1865. He weighed 171 pounds when he was captured, but upon his discharge he weighed only 73 pounds. After his discharge, Staples received a small government disability pension.

In the 1870 U.S. census, Francis and Orthelia were living with Francis's parents in Williamstown. In the 1880 U.S. census, Francis and Orthelia were living in their own house in Williamstown and had two children: Clarissa R., born on October 21, 1869, and Edward H., born on July 12, 1870. The census listed his occupation as farmer. Sometime in the early 1880s, a clerk in the U.S. Pension Bureau discovered that Staples had joined the Confederate army while in captivity and canceled his pension. He fought with the bureau for several years, but to no avail. Finally, Staples contacted Vermont senator Redfield Proctor, who got Staples's thirty-dollar-a-month pension reinstated.

For some unknown reason, Francis traveled around the nation during the last few years of his life without his family. In 1899, he was admitted to the Danville Branch of the National Home for Disabled Volunteer Soldiers in

Danville, Illinois. That same year, he was admitted to the Pacific Branch in Santa Monica, California. In 1903, he was admitted to the Southern Branch in Hampton, Virginia. Francis Staples died on August 17, 1909, and was buried in site 9, row D, section 16, at the Los Angeles National Cemetery in Los Angeles, California.[97]

Milton Bigelow Staples

Company E

Milton B. Staples, son of Isaac S. and Rhoda Dickinson Staples and older brother of Francis H. Staples, was born in Williamstown on January 15, 1840. He enlisted in Company E, 8th Vermont Infantry Regiment, in Williamstown on January 6, 1862. At the time of his enlistment, he had blue eyes, brown hair and stood five feet, six inches tall. He listed his occupation as a laborer. He was mustered out of service on June 28, 1865. Sometime after the war, Milton moved to Corinth, Vermont, where he farmed. Milton Staples never married and died on July 3, 1921. He was buried at Corinth Center Cemetery. The cause of death was aortic regurgitation, arteriosclerosis and high blood pressure. He was eighty-one years old.[98]

Daniel G. Webster

Company C

Daniel G. Webster enlisted in Company B, 4th Vermont Infantry Regiment, on August 17, 1861, in Chelsea, Vermont. He was discharged for a disability on November 5, 1862. After recovering from his illness, he enlisted in Company C, 8th Vermont Infantry Regiment, on August 15, 1864, and received a $600 town bounty. He served out his enlistment without further incident and was mustered out on June 1, 1865. Sometime after leaving the army, Daniel and his wife, Mary, moved west to Minnesota. Daniel died there of typhoid fever on January 16, 1884, and was buried at Oak Grove Cemetery, Detroit Lakes, Minnesota. At the time of his death, he was receiving an $8-a-month government disability pension. Mary applied for a widow's pension but was turned down in

1886. The pension bureau rejected her claim, stating that typhoid had nothing to do with his epilepsy. Mary responded that one doctor claimed he died of typhoid fever, while two others claimed it was from epileptic fits. She appealed but lost (see p. 46).[99]

Charles A. White Jr.

Company C

Charles A. White, born in 1816, enlisted in Company D, 2nd Vermont Infantry Regiment, in Williamstown on May 7, 1861, at age forty-eight and was selected as corporal. He was wounded in the leg at the Battle of Fredericksburg on December 13, 1862. He was mustered out on June 29, 1864, at the expiration of his enlistment. Somehow, in spite of his leg wound, Charles enlisted again a month later on August 30, 1864, in Company C, 8th Vermont Infantry Regiment, and received a $600 town bounty. He was mustered out of service on June 1, 1865. After the war, Charles White moved west, finally settling in Newkirk, Oklahoma. The $2-a-month government disability pension he received after the war seemed to be sufficient. However, by 1905 his right leg was contracted to the point that he could no longer work, and he asked for a pension increase. His military pension record has a number of documents pertaining to the argument for his case, but there is no evidence that he got an increase.[100]

11

9th VERMONT INFANTRY REGIMENT

The 9th Vermont Infantry Regiment was mustered into service in Brattleboro on July 9, 1862, and reported for duty in Washington, D.C., on July 17. The regiment was soon assigned to the Army of Virginia, and on July 27 the Vermonters arrived in Winchester, Virginia, where they would remain until September 2, when Confederate forces caused them to relocate to Harpers Ferry. While at Harpers Ferry, the 9th Vermont, along with the other units there, were attacked by an overwhelming Confederate force, and the Union commander surrendered. After being paroled, the Harpers Ferry units were sent to Chicago to guard Confederate prisoners of war. After being exchanged, in April 1863, the 9th Vermont was sent to Suffolk, Virginia, where it participated in the Siege of Suffolk. In August, it was sent across Hampton Roads to garrison Yorktown. In the intense Virginia heat, the Vermonters suffered from malaria and other diseases, killing a number of them. In January 1864, the commander of the 9th Vermont got his regiment transferred to a healthier climate at Newport Barracks, North Carolina, near New Bern. Here, the 9th Vermont was hit by a large Confederate force on February 2, forcing it to retreat. The rest of the Vermonters' time at Newport Barracks was uneventful. The 9th Vermont was transferred to the Army of the Potomac in Virginia; it arrived at Petersburg on September 17. On September 30, the 9th Vermont participated in the Battle of Fort Harrison below Richmond and successfully captured a Rebel fortification. The 9th Vermont was mustered out of service on December 1, 1865.[101]

Silas Burke Bohonon

Company I

Silas B. Bohonon, son of Alfred and Luceba Crook Bohonon, was born on May 12, 1825. He married Permilia R. Kingsbury in Lowell, Massachusetts, on December 9, 1851. Silas enlisted in Company I, 9th Vermont Infantry Regiment, in Chelsea, Vermont, on August 6, 1864. He was mustered out of service on June 13, 1865. After the war, Silas bought a farm in Williamstown on top of the hill in what is now Ainsworth State Park. In June 1879, Silas and his son, Willie, got into a bit of a scrape. For some reason, while in Barre in June 1879, Willie held a man named Henry Ketchum while Silas beat him up. Silas was arrested on June 16 and taken to Barre to answer to a charge of assault and battery. The outcome of the case is unknown. The next year, Willie was committed to the Asylum for the Insane in Brattleboro. Silas died of lead poisoning in Williamstown on July 21, 1885, at age sixty and was buried at Williamstown's Village Cemetery. Permilia applied for a veteran widow's pension in 1887 but for some reason never completed all the necessary paperwork and never received the pension.[102]

Orvis K. Marston

Company I

Orvis K. Marston was born in Fairlee, Vermont, on October 8, 1811. He married Caroline Litch of Wolcott, Vermont, on December 9, 1838, in Williamstown. Orvis was the father of Chester C. Marston, who was in Company D, 12th Vermont, and William L. Marston, who was in Company I, 9th Vermont. Orvis Marston enlisted in Company I, 9th Vermont Infantry Regiment, in Williamstown on December 29, 1863, at the age of fifty-two and received a $315 bounty from the town. He joined his son, William L. Marston, who had enlisted in Company I on June 24, 1862, at Newport Barracks, North Carolina. Orvis was hospitalized in Newport Barracks in August 1864 for chronic diarrhea and fever until he was shipped to Point of Rocks Military Hospital in Petersburg, Virginia, where he stayed for six weeks. Then he was given a furlough to go home. He returned to his regiment seventeen days later. Orvis was hospitalized in August 1865 and remained there until he was discharged on December 1, 1865. Orvis and Caroline lived in Williamstown until 1869, when they moved to Barnston, Canada, where Orvis farmed. In 1872, they moved to Troy, New York, where Orvis died on April 16, 1885. He was buried at Newport Center Cemetery in Newport, Vermont. After his death, Caroline received a veteran's widow pension until she died on October 3, 1909, in Troy.[103]

William L. Marston

Company I

William L. Marston, son of Orvis K. and Caroline Litch Marston, was born in Williamstown in 1845. He enlisted in Company I, 9th Vermont Infantry Regiment, on June 24, 1862, at age seventeen. He stood five feet, six inches tall and listed his occupation as a farmer. He was wounded on September 29, 1864, at the Battle of Chapin's Farm, just south of Richmond, Virginia, where a Minié ball struck him on the outside of his right heel. After being evacuated down the James River by steamboat, he was admitted to the Chesapeake General Hospital in Hampton, Virginia, on October 10, 1864. On October 15, he was admitted to a hospital in Pennsylvania. Then he was evacuated to Vermont, where, on November 5, he was admitted to the Governor Smith General Hospital in Brattleboro. He was mustered out of service on June 13, 1865. William married Jennie S. Bailey on May 9, 1874, in Dover, New Hampshire. She had previously been married to William's brother, Chester G. Marston, who served in Company D, 12th Vermont Infantry Regiment. Chester drowned in a millpond on April 22, 1874, at Great Falls (present-day Somersworth), New Hampshire. William died on February 15, 1918, and was buried at Highland Cemetery in Chelsea, Vermont.[104]

LaRoy Sunderland Norris

Company I

LaRoy S. Norris, son of Laban C. and Damaris Parsons Norris, was born on February 15, 1838. The Norrises moved from Corinth, Vermont, to Williamstown when LaRoy was very young. He enlisted in Company I, 9th Vermont Infantry Regiment, in Williamstown on January 4, 1864, and received a $315 town bounty. He was mustered out of service on May 13, 1865. After the war, Norris returned to Williamstown and lived with his parents on the family farm. LaRoy married Harriet Isabell Sheffield in 1876. She was the daughter of James H. and Hudah Sheffield and was from Ausable Forks, New York. Norris received a $3-a-month government disability pension for fever, ague, chronic diarrhea and chronic cough. Harriet died of heart disease on October 7, 1881, at age thirty-six and was buried at Williamstown's East Hill Cemetery. LaRoy next married Mary M. Shurtleff, daughter of Otis and Miranda Shurtleff of Berlin, Vermont, on November 26, 1885, in Williamstown. Sometime between 1885 and 1890, LaRoy built a house in Barre, where he and Mary lived for the rest of their lives. LaRoy died of heart disease in Barre on December 31, 1916, at age seventy-eight and was buried in Williamstown's East Hill Cemetery. Mary died in 1926 and was buried beside her husband. According to an article in the *Williamstown Herald*, she had "been hopelessly demented for many years."[105]

Charles H. Perry

Company F

Charles H. Perry, son of Heman G. and Betsy Perry, was born on May 18, 1845, in Williamstown. He enlisted in Company I, 13th Vermont Infantry Regiment, in Barre, Vermont, on August 25, 1862. His father, Heman Perry, served in Company D, 15th Vermont Infantry Regiment. Charles H. Perry was mustered out of service with his regiment on July 21, 1863. He enlisted in Company F, 9th Vermont Infantry Regiment, in Orange, Vermont, on January 2, 1864. He was promoted to corporal on June 29, 1864, and to sergeant on March 17, 1865. He was transferred to Company B on June 13, 1865, and was promoted to first sergeant on June 19, 1865. Charles was mustered out of service on December 1, 1865. After the war, Charles married Mary A. Carpenter in Williamstown on December 14, 1870. Mary died of tuberculosis on December 6, 1900, at age forty-eight and was buried at Williamstown's Village Cemetery. Charles died of diabetes in his home on April 14, 1901, at age fifty-four and was buried beside his wife (see p. 124).[106]

Lorenzo D. Smith

Company G

Lorenzo D. Smith, son of Norman Smith, was born in Brookfield, Vermont, on December 3, 1815. He married Sarah E. Gleason and resided in Warren, Vermont, for about twenty years. Lorenzo and Sarah raised a family of five children: Alonzo, Warren, Helen M., Julia E. and Laura S. Laura S. Smith married Ralph Ditty, who served in Company F, 2nd Vermont, and lived in Williamstown after the war. Smith enlisted in Company G, 9th Vermont Infantry Regiment, in Randolph, Vermont, on December 30, 1863, at age forty-eight; he was much older than most men in his regiment. On June 21, 1864, at a skirmish near Jacksonville, North Carolina, a Rebel Minié ball took the wig off Smith's head without scratching his scalp. The wig, however, was ruined. He was admitted to Sloan General Hospital in Montpelier on March 1, 1865, for some type of disease and was mustered out of service on June 22, 1865. After the war, he lived in Williamstown.[107]

12

10th VERMONT INFANTRY REGIMENT

The 10th Vermont Infantry Regiment was mustered into service on September 1, 1862, in Brattleboro. It soon received orders to move south and, on September 6, arrived in Washington, D.C. The regiment's first engagement was on November 27, 1863, at Orange Grove, Virginia, where it lost thirteen men killed and fifty-seven wounded. The next year, the 10th Vermont fought in the Battles of the Wilderness, Spotsylvania, Cold Harbor and the Weldon Railroad. On July 6, 1864, the 10th Vermont was ordered to Harpers Ferry, Virginia, but while passing through Frederick, Maryland, it was ordered, along with the rest of its brigade, to report to Major General Lew Wallace to help protect the nation's capital against Lieutenant General Jubal A. Early's fifteen-thousand-man army. On July 9, Wallace's cobbled-together force met Early's overwhelming number of Rebels on the south side of the Monocacy River, several miles below Frederick. Although defeated, Wallace's men heroically held off the Rebels long enough for other units to be sent to Washington. After Monocacy, the 10th Vermont fought in the Shenandoah Valley at Winchester, Fisher's Hill and Cedar Creek. On December 3, the 10th Vermont, along with the rest of the Sixth Corps, was ordered to Petersburg to join the rest of the Army of the Potomac. Here, the Vermonters fought at the final breakthrough at Petersburg and Sailor's Creek. The 10th Vermont was mustered out on June 27, 1865.[108]

IRA J. BADGER

Company G

Ira J. Badger married Mabel A. Woolcut in Williamstown on November 15, 1855. Mabel was the daughter of James and Betsy Woolcut of Williamstown. Ira and Mabel had one child, Alfred Martin Badger, born in Williamstown on November 20, 1859. Ira Badger enlisted in Company G, 10th Vermont Infantry Regiment, in Williamstown on August 8, 1862, at age twenty-seven. He was slightly wounded on June 1, 1864, at the Battle of Cold Harbor on the outskirts of Richmond, Virginia. On October 19, 1864, Badger was killed in the Battle of Cedar Creek in Virginia's Shenandoah Valley. After Ira's death, Mabel married Wilder S. Drew on November 28, 1866, and they lived in Fayston, Vermont. Mabel had been receiving a government widow's pension, but it stopped when she married Wilder. Alfred received a pension starting on November 29, 1866, and continued until he turned sixteen.[109]

ALMON CLARK BOUTWELL

Company G

Almon C. Boutwell, son of Samuel P. and Lydia Allen Boutwell, was born in Williamstown on June 15, 1846. He enlisted in Company G, 10th Vermont Infantry Regiment, in Williamstown on August 4, 1862. When he enlisted, he was sixteen years old and stood five feet, nine inches tall. He had a light complexion, blue eyes and light hair and listed his occupation as a farmer. Boutwell was promoted to corporal on January 1, 1864. The following summer, he was wounded on June 1 at the Battle of Cold Harbor on the outskirts of Richmond, Virginia, where a Rebel Minié ball entered his right shoulder just inside and below the head of the humerus. The bullet passed beneath the clavicle and exited through his right shoulder blade, shattering bones in its course. He was in several hospitals between Richmond and Washington, D.C., before being evacuated to Sloan General Hospital in Montpelier. Because of the severity of his wound, he was given a disability discharge on January 27, 1865. On October 17, 1870, Almon Boutwell married Abbie Josephine Morse in Pittsfield, Vermont. She was the daughter of Isaac Austin Morse and Helen Shedd Morse and was born in Sherburne, Vermont, on February 22, 1852. Almon and Abbie had no children of their own but adopted a boy, whom they named Clinton Wilbur Boutwell. Clinton was born on March 26, 1876. Almon became the proprietor of the Combination Cash Store at 40 Stratton Road in Rutland and was active in the Roberts Post, No. 14, of the Grand Army of the Republic, a Civil War veterans organization. Almon Boutwell died of heart disease in Rutland at midnight on April 25, 1906, at age fifty-nine. He was buried at Evergreen Cemetery in Rutland on April 29, 1906.

Abbie Boutwell died in Kendallville, Indiana, at 6:30 a.m. on June 12, 1933, while returning from a trip to California with family. She had a heart attack in the car and died almost immediately at age eighty-three. She was buried at Center Rutland Cemetery on June 17, 1933. Almon and Abbie's son, Clinton, became a medical doctor and married Charlotte Parker. They had one child, who was born in 1903. They named him Almon Otis Boutwell after his grandfather. Clinton Boutwell died in 1943.[110]

Henry P. Burnham

Company G

Henry P. Burnham, son of David and Betsy Olds Burnham of Williamstown, was born on December 17, 1843. He enlisted as a private in Company G, 10th Vermont Infantry Regiment, in Williamstown on August 5, 1862, at the age of nineteen. Burnham was shot through the head and died instantly on October 19, 1864, at the Battle of Cedar Creek in Virginia's Shenandoah Valley. He was buried on the field near where he fell. Someone from Burnham's family, probably Henry's father, went to Cedar Creek and brought his body back to Williamstown for burial. The funeral was held on Sunday afternoon, November 20, 1864, at the Congregational church, Reverend Pliny F. Barnard presiding. He was buried at Williamstown's East Hill Cemetery.

The following was Henry P. Burnham's obituary in the *Walton Daily Journal* on November 15, 1864:

A Fallen Hero

> *The following tribute to private Henry P. Burnham, Co. G., 10th Vermont Regiment, son of David Burnham, Esq., of Williamstown, is furnished by an officer of his acquaintance and will be read with*

more than ordinary interest, and afford much comfort to the numerous relatives and friends of the family: "Our brigade had made a charge and retaken McKnight's guns on the morning of Oct. 19th, and the enemy being on either flank was retreating rapidly to avoid being captured, when it received a volley from the flank, and privates Burnham and Crocker were instantly killed—both shot through the head, evidently by the same bullet, and fell forward upon their faces, neither of them speaking after being struck. It would have been folly for any man to have waited there long enough to take their effects, so they were left; and the rebels, who were on the ground the next minute, got them. When the men of his company got his body the morning after the battle, everything had been taken away except his clothing, and even his boots and stockings were gone. No one in his company has any property belonging to him, consequently I cannot send you any memento of him from the field. But you have assurances from his officers, and from all of his comrades that he was an excellent soldier, intelligent, patient, faithful and brave, among the foremost in the advance, and the last to retreat, never seeking to avoid duty, always in his place. I have seen him meekly bearing his burden when exhausted by loss of sleep, excessive fatigue and the summer's heat, marching bravely onward with the column through clouds of dust, and never complaining or faltering, until the work was done. But his marches are all over, his hard work is done and his name is inscribed on the roll of heroes." The funeral service of the above named soldier will occur at the Congregational Church, in Williamstown, on Sunday afternoon Nov. 20th. The friends of the family and his brother soldiers are especially invited to attend.

The following letters concerning the death and burial of Henry P. Burnham are from the collections of the Vermont Historical Society:

10th Vt. Vols.
Near Middletown, Va.
Nov 6, 1864

Dear Sir:

Your letter of the 31st ult. Requesting information concerning the death of your brother-in-law arrived this evening's mail.

He was killed instantly on the morning of Oct. 19th about one fourth of a mile from where our regiment is now encamped…

He was buried with the others of his company who were killed in this battle, near where he fell. The bodies can be removed without difficulty, and if the gentleman to whom you referred comes to do it I will gladly render him all the assistance in my power. You have my thanks for the complimentary manner in which you mention my letters to the Journal, *and also for your offer to send it to me. I will write whenever there is anything of interest to communicate, but you need not consider your self obliged to send the paper for I already have the reading of it.*

Hoping this letter affords you all the information you desire and that it may be of some consolation to you.

I am very respectfully,
Your obdt. Servt.
Almon Clark

Almon Clark, of Barre, was the assistant surgeon of the 10th Vermont Infantry Regiment, and this letter was written to Henry P. Burnham's father, David Burnham. The Crocker who was mentioned was Private Charles H. Crocker from Brookfield, Vermont, also a member of Company G, 10th Vermont Infantry.

Camp Russell Virginia Nov 13th, 1864

Mr. Burnham

Dear Sir. Yours of the 12th is at hand, and in reply I will say that the body of your son was robbed by the rebels they getting possession of the ground where he fell soon after he was killed and held it until near night. They took every thing but his shirt and pants.

He was instantly killed being shot through the head by a musket ball.

He was killed between the hours of eight and nine A.M. The articles you mention as being sent to him were received by Sergeant Ingram and disposed of by him. The boys are all out of money now, but I will collect the pay for them as soon as we are paid again and forward it to you. The trouble as far as I am concerned will be nothing.

I shall be happy to assist you in any way that is in my power.

Very respectfully
Thomas H. White

This letter was written by Sergeant H. White of Topsham, Company G, 10th Vermont, to Henry P. Burnham's father, David Burnham. Sergeant Ingram is Almon Ingram of Washington, Vermont.

Williamstown Nov. 13. 1864

Winslow & Martha

We have decided to have Henry's funeral sermon preached next Sunday, Nov. 20th. It will be attended at the Congregationalist Meetinghouse as Rev. P.F. Barnard will preach. We received a letter from Sergt. Thomas H. White of Co. G 10th Vt. saying that Henry was killed in the great battle of the 19th & died in the front ranks nobly doing his duty. This all he wrote about him but said if we wished any information respecting him he would cheerfully give it.

Whenever Aunt Eunice wishes to come home or you get ready to have her come I suppose you will let us know it & we will endeavor to go for her. It is quite wintery here this morning.

If Martha has not written to Henry's folks yet about the card she must do so soon as they wish to sell it if she does not want it as they can sell it at West Randolph for .25 pr. lb. or you can have it at that price only they want to know what to do about it immediately.

Helen Martin was buried last Thursday. Widow Joshua Burnham (Eofa Martin, Mosely Martin's sister, Aunt Eunice will know who she was) was buried Wednesday, but I can't give dates or ages.

Emma Burnham[111]

LEANDER DECAMP

Company G

Leander Decamp enlisted in Company G, 10th Vermont Infantry Regiment, in Williamstown on August 8, 1862, and was wounded on June 3, 1864, at the Battle of Cold Harbor, Virginia. He was shot in both hands and the right shoulder. He was first sent to the Sixth Corps Hospital at White House Landing and then to a hospital in Washington, D.C. He died of his wounds on June 14, 1864. Leander's father, John Decamp, applied for a government pension because Leander was his sole support, but he died before he received it. John Decamp died on March 13, 1879, in East Burke. Leander's stepmother, Sarah, applied for a pension after John Decamp died and received an eight-dollar-a-month pension starting in 1892. John Decamp had originally married Aurslia Cutler of Montpelier, in Montpelier, on January 5, 1834. After Aurslia died, he married Sarah W. Webster in St. Johnsbury on September 8, 1850.[112]

George G. Edson

Company G

George G. Edson enlisted in Company B, 6th Vermont Infantry Regiment, in Williamstown on October 3, 1861. He was given a disability discharge for disease on May 21, 1862. After recovering from his illness, he enlisted in Company G, 10th Vermont Infantry Regiment, in Williamstown on August 29, 1864, for which he received a $600 bounty from the town. Edson was killed in action on October 19, 1864, at the Battle of Cedar Creek, Virginia. He was buried at the National Cemetery in Winchester, Virginia (see p. 56).[113]

Gardner Fay

Company I

Gardner Fay was born on October 4, 1829, in Calais, Vermont. After he finished his education, he trained as a carpenter. He married Matilda Catherine Sancry on June 22, 1854, in Boston, Massachusetts. They had three sons: Allard G., born on December 4, 1856, in Brookfield; Frank I., born on October 1, 1859, in Williamstown; and Elmer W. Gardner, born on December 8, 1861, in Williamstown. At the outbreak of the Civil War, Gardner Fay and his family were living in Williamstown, where he enlisted in Company I, 10th Vermont Infantry Regiment, on August 1, 1862, at age thirty-two. He was promoted to corporal on November 16, 1862. A year later, on November 27, 1863, Fay was killed in the Battle of Orange Grove in Orange County, Virginia, during what would later be known as the Mine Run Campaign. After Gardner's death, Matilda received a government widow's pension of eight dollars a month, and each of her three boys received two dollars a month until they reached the age of sixteen. Matilda married Edson K. Allen on December 28, 1876, in Montpelier. It was the second marriage for both. Of course, Matilda had to give up her pension when she married Edson. Matilda died on December 18, 1892. Allard G. Fay became a lawyer and judge and resided for most of his life in Barre, Vermont. Frank I. Fay became a watchmaker and jeweler in Willimantic, Connecticut. Elmer W. Fay became a blacksmith in North Attleboro, Massachusetts.[114]

LEWIS W. FLINT

Company G

Lewis W. Flint, born on July 15, 1838, enlisted in Company G, 10th Vermont Infantry Regiment, in Williamstown on December 29, 1863, and received a $315 town bounty. He was mustered out of service on June 17, 1865. Lewis Flint returned to Williamstown after the war. He died of heart disease on July 15, 1886, and was buried at Williamstown's Village Cemetery.[115]

DENNISON L. HOPKINS

Company G

Eighteen-year-old Dennison L. Hopkins enlisted in Company G, 10th Vermont Infantry Regiment, in Williamstown on August 8, 1862, and was promoted to corporal on September 1, 1862. He was shot in the left shoulder on June 3, 1864, in the second charge at Cold Harbor on the outskirts of Richmond, Virginia. He was evacuated back to the Judiciary Square General Hospital in Washington, D.C., where he died of blood poisoning on June 25. His mother, Eliza M. Hopkins, received an eight-dollar-a-month dependent mother's government pension starting on May 2, 1866.[116]

Perry Hopkins

Company G

Perry Hopkins was born in Williamstown on February 28, 1830. He married Elvira Melinda Simons on March 15, 1855, in Williamstown. They had one child, John P. Hopkins, born on May 3, 1857. Hopkins enlisted in Company G, 10th Vermont Infantry Regiment, at age thirty-three in Williamstown on December 10, 1863, and received a $315 town bounty. When he enlisted, he stood five feet, eight inches tall. He had blue eyes and brown hair and listed his occupation as a farmer. On May 12, 1864, Perry was in the Battle of Spotsylvania Court House, where he received a serious but embarrassing wound. He was hit by a Rebel Minié ball in the buttocks. The bullet entered the right buttock and exited out of the left one. With the bullet went quite a bit of muscle, causing him to have trouble walking even after the wound healed. He was in military hospitals for six months until he was mustered out of service on June 29, 1865. Shortly after the war, Hopkins and his family moved to Eagleton, Wisconsin, where he operated a hotel known as the Nine Mile House, a popular stopping place for lumbermen on their way to and from the woods. Because of his jovial and caring nature, he was known as "Uncle Perry." He later moved to nearby Bloomer, about six miles northwest of Eagleton. This was probably after the death of his wife.

Starting in 1888, Perry received a six-dollar-a-month government disability pension for his gunshot wound in the buttocks, rheumatism, heart disease and senility. Elvira Hopkins died on October 2, 1896. Perry died on Monday, April 6, 1914, in Bloomer and was buried beside his wife on April 8 at the O'Neill Cemetery in Eagleton. He was escorted from the funeral services at the United Brethren Church to the cemetery by his GAR comrades. As a testament to his good nature, the following is from his obituary in the April 11, 1914 edition of the *Eau Claire Leader*:

> *He was the friend of the woodsman, as a farmer and citizen when he always fearlessly championed the course of righteousness and justice, he had made himself more than a local figure and his death is an irreparable loss to the entire community.*[117]

DAVID M. JILLSON

Company G

David M. Jillson, son of Isaac and Hannah C. Jillson, was born in Williamstown. Isaac Jillson was disabled by a hernia on his right side, and the family was so poor that the town bought them a small farm in 1843 just so they could survive. Their daughter, Elvira H. Jillson, who was working in Manchester, New Hampshire, bought the house from the town for her parents in 1857. David enlisted in Company G, 10th Vermont Infantry Regiment, in Williamstown on July 30, 1862, at age nineteen. After he enlisted, David let his parents have his state pay of seven dollars a month. David Jillson was wounded three times while he was in the army. He was first wounded at the Battle of Cold Harbor on June 1, 1864. He was wounded again on September 19, 1864, at the Battle of Winchester. He received his last wound at the Union breakthrough at Petersburg, Virginia, on April 2, 1865. He was mustered out of service on June 22, 1865. David Jillson died on December 30, 1865, at age twenty-two in Pomfret, Vermont, of chronic diarrhea that he had contracted in the army. His body was brought back to Williamstown and was buried at East Hill Cemetery. David's mother applied for a government dependent mother's pension after his death. The pension was approved, and she received an eight-dollar-a-month pension backdated to December 31, 1865. In the last year of their lives, Isaac and Hannah were so feeble that David's sister, Elvira, quit her job in New Hampshire and returned to Williamstown to take care of them. Both Isaac and Hannah died on the same day, August 26, 1870.[118]

LOREN G. KIDDER

Company G

Loren G. Kidder was born in Randolph, Vermont, on February 5, 1834. He enlisted in Company G, 10th Vermont Infantry Regiment, in Randolph on August 9, 1862. The next day, Kidder married Nancy Evans. In July 1863, he suffered sunstroke while on a long march. Then, on November 27, 1863, in the Battle of Orange Grove, Virginia, Kidder was hit in the head by a Rebel Minié ball. The ball carried away part of his skull, and after it healed, he had memory problems. He went back to his regiment, but because of the severity of his wound, on June 15, 1864, he was transferred to the Veteran Reserve Corps, where he remained until he mustered out of service on July 3, 1865. After his return from the army, he and Nancy had three children: Agnes M., born on February 8, 1867; Hattie R., born on April 29, 1872; and Harry M., born on February 23, 1879. By 1888, Loren was in bad shape and applied for a government disability pension. He suffered from headaches, impaired vision and rheumatism so bad he could do very little manual labor. His hands shook so much that he could hardly feed himself. For all these ailments, he did receive a small disability pension. Nancy died in Northfield on October 5, 1904. Loren next married Ellen Douglas Rennie in Peacham, Vermont, on June 28, 1911. Loren died in Peacham on August 17, 1917. After his death, Ellen Kidder moved to Barboursville, Virginia. She died in Western State Hospital, a facility for the insane in Staunton, Virginia.[119]

Charles Gastings Newton

Company G

Charles G. Newton, son of David and Sarah Newton, was born in Rochester, Vermont, on August 8, 1837. His family was not of means, and after finishing public school, he taught school in the fall and spring terms and worked as a farmhand in the summer to earn enough money to further his education. He attended Barre Academy in preparation to attend Middlebury College, which he did in 1861. In July 1862, with the president's call for more troops, he left college and assisted in recruiting for the 10th Vermont Infantry Regiment. After the regiment was formed, Newton was commissioned as the second lieutenant of Company G on August 12,

Charles G. Newton, Company G, 10th Vermont Infantry Regiment. *Courtesy of the Vermont Historical Society.*

1862. He listed his residence as Williamstown, Vermont, but no record of Newton's living in Williamstown can be found. It is possible that he made friends in Williamstown while attending the Barre Academy. Lieutenant Newton was in every battle with his regiment. On June 1, 1864, during the Battle of Cold Harbor, Virginia, the 10th Vermont was charging Confederate positions, and as it halted for a moment to allow other regiments to catch up, Newton noticed Rebels on the 10th's flank and exclaimed, "I see the scamps! I see them!" At that moment, a Rebel Minié ball slit his throat, and he dropped to the ground and bled to death within minutes. Newton's comrades buried him the next day near where he fell on the battlefield. His grave was located under a mulberry and sassafras tree that grew up strangely into a common trunk. His family had his body removed and reinterred at the North Hollow Cemetery in Rochester, Vermont.[120]

GEORGE L. POOR

Company G

George L. Poor, son of John and Susan Poor, was born in Williamstown on January 24, 1843. He enlisted in Company G, 10th Vermont Infantry Regiment, in Williamstown on August 4, 1862, at age nineteen. He stood five feet, nine and a half inches tall and had blue eyes and brown hair. He listed his occupation as a farmer. George Poor was wounded on July 9, 1864, at the Battle of Monocacy, Maryland. He was hit in the right forearm about two inches below the elbow by a Rebel Minié ball. The bullet shattered his ulna before exiting, leaving his arm almost useless. He was admitted to Patterson Park General Hospital (also known as General Hospital No. 7) in Baltimore on July 10, 1864. Sometime later, he was transferred to Sloan General Hospital in Montpelier. Poor was given a disability discharge

George L. Poor, Company G, 10th Vermont Infantry Regiment, displaying his wound to the U.S. Pension Bureau. *Courtesy of the National Archives.*

at Sloan General Hospital on August 31, 1865. He received the disability discharge for the wound in his right arm, gangrene and necrosis of the ulna (death of the bone). In 1866, pieces of bone were still working their way out of his arm, and he was never again able to extend the fingers of his right hand. Upon his discharge from the army, he received a four-dollar-a-month government disability pension. On March 28, 1867, his pension was increased to eight dollars a month. George Poor died on July 25, 1870, at age twenty-seven and was buried at Williamstown's Village Cemetery. He never married.[121]

Ira Allen Rice

Company G

Ira A. Rice was born on October 8, 1829, in Stockholm, New York. He enlisted in Company G, 10th Vermont Infantry Regiment, in Williamstown on July 30, 1862. At the time of his enlistment, he stood five feet, ten and a half inches tall and listed his occupation as a farmer. Rice deserted on May 13, 1864, near Spotsylvania Court House, Virginia. He surrendered to the provost martial in Potsdam, New York, on May 5, 1865, and under a presidential proclamation of amnesty he was honorably discharged on May 13, 1865. After returning from the army, Ira married Ruth S. Davenport on November 27, 1865, in Brookfield, Vermont. They had six children, three born in Williamstown and three born in Wisconsin. Ira divorced Ruth on September 19, 1895, in Florence, Wisconsin. He next married Mary A. Parmenter on April 14, 1896, in Florence. She had previously been married to Dana Parmenter on April 19, 1881, in Portage, Wisconsin. Dana Parmenter died on June 15, 1895, of a cerebral hemorrhage. In 1912, Ira's pension was raised to thirty dollars a month for a hernia and rheumatism. He died in Florence on August 7, 1915, at age eighty-five.[122]

Joseph Kingsbury Williams Jr.

Company G

Joseph K. Williams Jr., son of Joseph K. and Mary B. Williams, was born in Williamstown on April 13, 1840. He enlisted in Company G, 10th Vermont Infantry Regiment, in Williamstown on August 11, 1862. He was wounded by a Rebel Minié ball on June 3, 1864, at Cold Harbor in Richmond, Virginia, and died of his wound on June 5. His mother and father were dependent on Joseph for their support, and when his father died on July 13, 1868, his mother applied for a government pension. Her application was approved on January 20, 1873.[123]

George W. Wise

Company G

George W. Wise was born in Elizabethtown, New York, on April 21, 1842. He enlisted in Company G, 10th Vermont Infantry Regiment, in Williamstown on July 30, 1862. He was promoted to corporal on September 13, 1863. Wise was wounded in the right hand on April 2, 1865, at the breakthrough at Petersburg. He was admitted to the army hospital at City Point, Virginia, and then transferred to Finley Hospital in Washington, D.C., where he was mustered out of service on June 12, 1865. After the war, he lived in Barre for some time. He received a government disability pension later in life for his hand wound and chronic diarrhea. Then, in 1907, his health deteriorated to such an extent that he could not take care of himself, and he moved in with a niece in Saranac Lake, New York. George Wise died there on January 28, 1923. At the time of his death, he was receiving a fifty-dollar-a-month government disability pension.[124]

13

11TH VERMONT INFANTRY REGIMENT

The 11th Vermont Infantry Regiment was mustered into service in Brattleboro on September 1, 1862. It shipped out for Washington, D.C., on September 7 and arrived there on the ninth. Within days of arriving in Washington, the 11th Vermont was redesignated the 1st Vermont Heavy Artillery and spent the next year and a half in the forts that ringed the nation's capital. There, the Vermonters learned to become artillerymen and built fortifications. At the start of Lieutenant General Ulysses S. Grant's spring campaign of 1864, the 1st Vermont Heavy Artillery reverted back to infantry and was sent to the front in Virginia. The 11th Vermont was assigned to the Vermont Brigade and participated in its first battle on May 18 at Spotsylvania. The 11th Vermont fought in every battle with the Vermont Brigade until the end of the war, when it was mustered out of service on August 25, 1865.[125]

Horace B. Foster

Company L

Horace B. Foster enlisted in Company L, 11th Vermont Infantry Regiment, in Hardwick, Vermont, on May 15, 1863, and was selected as a corporal. He was taken prisoner on June 23, 1864, at the Battle of Weldon Railroad near Petersburg, Virginia, and was sent to the prisoner of war camp at

Horace B. Foster, Company L, 11th Vermont Infantry Regiment. *Courtesy of the U.S. Army Military History Institute.*

Andersonville, Georgia, where he died on May 20, 1865. There is a cenotaph for Horace B. Foster at Williamstown's Village Cemetery that reads, "Horace B. Foster (Cpl.), died September 7, 1864, age 24 years, 8 months, died at Andersonville, Ga., Bat. L, 11th Regt. Vt. Vols., son of William and Rebekka M. Foster." Horace Foster is buried in grave site 8201 in the national cemetery at Andersonville, Georgia.[126]

BARNEY RING

Company E

Barney Ring, son of Moses and Lucinda Ring, was born in Williamstown. At age twenty-three, he enlisted in Company E, 12th Vermont Infantry Regiment, in Williamstown on August 22, 1862. He measured five feet, ten inches tall and listed his occupation as a farmer. He had a dark complexion, black eyes and black hair. He was given a disability discharge on November 30, 1862, for typhoid fever, which also caused phthisis (wasting away) of his right testicle. After recovering from his illness, Ring enlisted in Company L, 11th Vermont Infantry Regiment, on June 26, 1863. He was mustered out of service on August 25, 1865. After returning to Williamstown, he married Mary Ann Bohonon in Washington, Vermont, on November 15, 1869. At the time of his marriage, Ring was living in Topsham, Vermont. It appears the couple did not stay together too long because in the 1870 U.S. census, Barney was living by himself in a boardinghouse in Lowell, Massachusetts. He and Mary Ann divorced in 1874.

Apparently, Barney Ring was quite a drinker. In the June 6, 1877 edition of the *Montpelier Argus and Patriot*, there appeared a humorous article about a visit Barney made to Vermont's capital city:

> *Monday last* [June 4] *Barney Ring of Peabody Station* [Massachusetts] *visited Montpelier, where he fell in with an old townsman—William*

> *Fellows, of Orange. The event had to be properly commemorated by "taking suthin." The result being that at an early hour in the afternoon "Barney" was compelled to "cool off" at the hotel de Dudley* [Montpelier jail]. *He hated to go, but the "tender solicitations" of several "minions of the law" proved too much for him. Fellows held out a while longer, but towards evening he, too, became garrulous, and, after a slight struggle was assisted to an apartment adjoining that of his companion. They were tenderly cared for until Tuesday forenoon, when, after a little examination, they were allowed to deposit a small sum to the credit of the State, tell where procured the wherewith to make them so salubrious and depart.*

In 1880, Barney was living in a boardinghouse in Roxbury, Vermont, and was working as a wood chopper. It must have been difficult to do that type of work since he was receiving a ten-dollar-a-month government disability pension for deafness, a shrunken right testicle and total blindness in his right eye, all caused by the typhoid fever and heart disease he contracted in the army. In September 1894, Ring was living in Northfield, Vermont, and on the fifteenth of that month he was admitted to the Vermont Soldiers' Home in Bennington. He died at the home on March 13, 1900. Since there were no relatives to claim the body, he was buried at what is now the Vermont Veterans' Home War Memorial Cemetery on the grounds of the home. He was the brother of William F. Ring, who served in Company C, 1st Vermont Cavalry Regiment.[127]

Edwin A. Wardwell

Company I

Edwin A. Wardwell, son of Isaac and Mary Cushing Wardwell, was born in Lebanon, New Hampshire, on August 13, 1827. He married Sylvia E. (maiden name unknown). They had two children: Mary E., born on May 15, 1853, in Brookfield, Vermont; and Inez M., born on September 25, 1865, in Williamstown. He enlisted in Company I, 11th Vermont Infantry Regiment, in Brookfield on August 8, 1862. He was transferred to the Veteran Reserve Corps on July 20, 1864, and was given a disability discharge on August 18, 1865. After his discharge, Edwin Wardwell settled in Williamstown, where he died of tuberculosis on March 1, 1866, at age thirty-eight. He was buried at Williamstown's Village Cemetery. After Edwin's death, Sylvia married a man named Osman Town on April 21, 1868.[128]

14
SECOND VERMONT BRIGADE

Because of the failure of Major General McClellan's attempt to capture Richmond, President Lincoln called for 300,000 militiamen in August 1862 to serve for nine months. The Federal government thought the war would be over by that time. Vermont's quota in this call was 4,898 troops. On August 12, the governor of Vermont activated all militia companies in the state. The next day, he issued a call for volunteers to fill out the activated companies. With this, the Second Vermont Brigade was formed consisting of the 12th, 13th, 14th, 15th and 16th Vermont Infantry Regiments under the command of Brigadier General Edwin H. Stoughton. The brigade came together in Washington, D.C., on October 29, 1862. Its mission for the next eight months was the defense of Washington, with most of its time spent in and around Fairfax Court House, Virginia.

During its stay in Virginia, the Second Vermont Brigade saw no combat; however, it did experience a raid led by Confederate captain John S. Mosby. Brigadier General Stoughton had established his headquarters several miles from his nearest regiment. Even though he had a small guard force, he was quite vulnerable, an opportunity not overlooked by Mosby. On the dark and rainy night of March 8, 1863, Mosby and thirty of his rangers captured several of Stoughton's guards, rode into Fairfax Court House and entered the hotel where Stoughton was living. Mosby knocked on Stoughton's door and announced that he had some dispatches for the general. The door was opened, and Mosby and several of his men quickly overcame the guards. They then went to Stoughton's bedroom, where Mosby supposedly awakened Stoughton by slapping him on the rump with the flat of his sword and informed him he was a prisoner. Mosby made off with the general, several of his aides, fifteen enlisted guards and fifty-five horses. President Lincoln said of the event that he did not so much mind the loss of a brigadier general, for he could make another one in five minutes, "but those horses cost $125 apiece." Stoughton spent the next three months in a prisoner of war camp in Richmond, Virginia, before he was exchanged.

After Stoughton's capture, Brigadier General George J. Stannard was put in command of the Second Vermont Brigade. On June 23, Stannard was notified that his brigade was assigned to the First Corps of the Army of the Potomac and that he was to be ready to march north with the army. On June 28, the Second Vermont Brigade commenced a grueling march in the summer heat to Gettysburg, Pennsylvania. After arriving in Gettysburg, the 12th and 15th Vermont were tagged to guard the First Corps wagon trains. The other three regiments continued on to the battle and were engaged on the second day, July 2. The brigade's greatest moment came on the third day of the battle, during Pickett's charge. As the Confederate charge neared the Union lines on Cemetery Ridge, Stannard ordered his regiments to hit the Confederate right flank. The assault was so fierce that it was key to stopping the Confederate charge. The regiments were mustered out of service just days after the battle, and the Second Vermont Brigade ceased to exist.[129]

15

12th Vermont Infantry Regiment

The 12th Vermont Infantry Regiment was mustered into service in Brattleboro on October 4, 1862. Its Company D was composed mainly of men from Williamstown, Chelsea and Tunbridge. It was mustered out of service on July 14, 1863.[130]

Cornelius N. Benedict

Company D

Cornelius N. Benedict, son of Squire and Adelia Rood Benedict of Williamstown, enlisted in Company D, 12th Vermont Infantry Regiment, on August 22, 1862. At the time of his enlistment, he was a twenty-three-year-old bachelor and listed his occupation as a farmer. Cornelius Benedict contracted an illness while protecting the capital and was hospitalized. He was given a disability discharge on April 22, 1863, for the effects of typhoid fever.[131]

Orville Howard Briggs

Company D

Orville H. Briggs, son of James Wright and Elvira Hatch Briggs of Williamstown, was born on March 14, 1838. He enlisted in Company D, 12th Vermont Infantry Regiment, in Williamstown on August 22, 1862. At the time of his enlistment, the twenty-four-year-old farmer stood five feet, six and a half inches tall and had blue eyes. He was mustered out of service with his regiment on July 14, 1863. Orville returned to Williamstown after his military service and went back to farming on South Hill Road. He married Ellen Mariah Putnam on January 16, 1864. They had one child, William Putnam Briggs, who was born on May 6, 1875. In December 1893, Orville applied for a government disability pension for ailments he contracted in the service. He was specifically troubled with sciatica in his left hip, rheumatism in his shoulders and heart trouble. He received a small pension until he died on April 14, 1896, of apoplexy. He was buried at Williamstown's East Hill Cemetery. After Orville's death, Ellen Briggs received a veteran widow's pension of forty dollars a month. Ellen died of arteriosclerosis and a cerebral thrombosis on February 23, 1936, six days after her ninety-fifth birthday. She was buried at East Hill Cemetery beside her husband.[132]

Orville H. Briggs, Company D, 12th Vermont Infantry Regiment. *Courtesy of Irene Walbridge.*

Photograph of the ring carved by Orville H. Briggs while in the army in northern Virginia. *Courtesy of Lila Walbridge.*

Henry Cram

Company D

Henry Cram was born in Williamstown on January 7, 1843. He enlisted in Company D, 12th Vermont Infantry Regiment, in Williamstown on August 22, 1862, and was mustered out of service with his regiment on July 14, 1863. Sometime after returning from the army, Cram moved to Barrington, Rhode Island, where, in 1872, he established a store. He later gained two partners and changed the name of the store to Ballou, Cram & Markham. They were dealers in furniture, carpets and house furnishings. They also sold crockery, glass, tin and woodenware. Although he was a successful businessman, he suffered from malaria and rheumatism, results of his military service, for which he received a small monthly government pension. Henry Cram died on October 1, 1921, and was buried at Prince's Cemetery in Barrington, Rhode Island.[133]

Henry W. Davis

Company D

After serving in the 1st Vermont Infantry Regiment, from May 2 to August 15, 1861, Henry W. Davis enlisted again in Williamstown and was commissioned a second lieutenant in Company D, 12th Vermont Infantry

Postwar photograph of Henry W. Davis, Company D, 1st, and Company D, 12th Vermont Infantry Regiments. *Courtesy of the Vermont Historical Society.*

Regiment, on August 23, 1862. He was discharged by special order of the War Department on February 7, 1863. Davis died on February 2, 1910, and was buried at Dellwood Cemetery in Manchester, Vermont (see p. 15).[134]

Horace S. Farnham

Company D

Horace S. Farnham, son of Aaron and Lydia Seaver Farnham of Williamstown, married Abbie S. Pope, of Brookfield, on March 4, 1862. She was the daughter of Edmund and Roxana Pope and was born in Brookfield in June 1835. Abbie died two months after her marriage, on May 9, 1862. Horace enlisted in Company D, 12th Vermont Infantry Regiment, in Williamstown on August 22, 1862, at age thirty-three. He served with his regiment for its nine-month tour of duty on the outskirts of Washington, D.C., where he was promoted to corporal on March 7, 1863. He was mustered out of service with his regiment on July 14, 1863. After returning to Williamstown, Farnham enlisted in Company C, 8th Vermont Infantry Regiment, in Williamstown on December 22, 1863 (see p. 69).[135]

JOHN FARNHAM

Company D

Postwar photograph of John and Laura Farnham. John served in Company D, 12th Vermont Infantry Regiment. *Courtesy of the Williamstown Historical Society.*

John Farnham was born on August 7, 1840, in Northfield, Vermont. He enlisted in Company D, 12th Vermont Infantry Regiment, in Williamstown on August 22, 1862, and listed his occupation as a farmer. He was mustered out of service on July 14, 1863. After his stint in the army, Farnham returned to Williamstown and resumed farming. He married Laura Martin Hatch, daughter of Reuben and Olive Martin Hatch, on December 20, 1866. He was twenty-six and she was eighteen. John Farnham died of heart disease on December 5, 1902, and was buried at Williamstown's Village Cemetery. Laura died of heart disease on February 1, 1917, in Barre at age sixty-eight and was buried beside her husband.[136]

NELSON FARNHAM

Company D

Nelson Farnham, son of Jonathan C. and Clarissa Worthington Farnham, was born in Williamstown on July 17, 1837. He farmed until he enlisted in Company D, 12th Vermont Infantry Regiment, in Williamstown on August 22, 1862. He was mustered out of service on July 14, 1863. Upon his return from the army, Nelson went back to farming. He married Martha Benedict of Williamstown on June 12, 1864. He died on March 29, 1889, and was buried at Elmwood Cemetery in Northfield.[137]

Newell Richard Farnham

Company D

Newell R. Farnham, son of Jonathan C. and Clarissa Worthington Farnham, was born in Williamstown on March 15, 1841. He enlisted in Company D, 12th Vermont Infantry Regiment, in Williamstown on August 22, 1862. He was mustered out of service with his regiment on July 14, 1863. He enlisted again on September 3, 1864, and received a $600 bounty from the town. Farnham got sick before he could be shipped south and was sent to Baxter General Hospital in Burlington, where he remained until he was discharged on April 28, 1865. It is unknown if he got to keep his bounty. After his discharge from the army, Newell returned to Williamstown and married Ella M. Braman, of Washington, Vermont, in 1872. They had one child, Herbert N. Farnham. Ella died of chronic nephritis and gallstones on September 18, 1910, at age fifty-eight and was buried at Williamstown's Village Cemetery. Newell died of arteriosclerosis on November 30, 1919, and was buried beside his wife.[138]

Henry Nathanial Jillson

Company D

Henry N. Jillson enlisted in Company D, 12th Vermont Infantry Regiment, in Williamstown on August 22, 1862, and was selected as first sergeant. He was mustered out of service with the rest of his regiment on July 14, 1863. The following are two letters written by Henry N. Jillson to his parents from Wolf Run Shoals, Virginia, in 1863:

Camp Near Wolf Run Shoals, Va.
Sunday, February 1, 1863

Dear Father:

I received a letter from you last night while on guard dated January 25th and was very happy to hear that you were well. My health is very good. We are having some wind now days it is awful it does not take more than 1 or 2 hours rain to make the mud knee deep. We moved from Fairfax the 20th of

Jany. and came way out here out of sight or hearing of anyone. the snow is about or has been the past week 6 or 7 inches deep but it is not cold at all. It seems some like spring. The box sent to Chester Marston came the 28th of Jan. I found some cookies, butter & sausage & I tell you it tasted good. Tell Mother I am very much obliged she could not have sent anything better. The butter did not taste like that miserable stuff that the sutler sells us for .50 cts. a lb. He asks for rasins 40 cts. per lb. For apples one large or two small ones for 5 cts. Now he can buy just as many as he is a mind to for $2.50 a barrel at Alexandria. For hand of tobacco such as we used to buy for 11 cts. he asks 35 cts. and other stuff in proportion.

I received a letter from Ellen the 30th she was well as usual. Also one from George House it was a good one too some ground advise in it. I have got most out of stockings and if you have a chance I wish you would send me a pair. We were paid off the 29th & received two months & ten days pay which makes up to the first of Nov. We expect to be paid up to the first of Jan. before too long. I know now what my pay is. I received for two months 10 ds $39.65. The Privates Received $30.33. We Williamstown Boys have each of us sent some home. The Capt. takes it to Washington for us & is going to send it by express to Genl. Bass. It is all together with paper enclosed stating the amount sent by each of us. I want you should take mine and do what you see fit with it. I sent $31.00. I had liked to have forgotten to tell you I received most if not all of the papers you sent me also that I recd. 14 postage stamps for all of which I am very thankful. But I cannot think of much more to write this time. So I will close by tendering to you and Mother my best wishes for the kindness you have bestowed upon me while in this strange land. So goodbye for this time from your son.

Henry N. Jillson

Camp near Wolf Run Shoals, Va.
April 13, 1863

Dear Mother & Father

I received your last in due time and was very glad to hear from you that you were well and prospering. I am enjoying the same continued good health though my companions are falling around me. We have had orders to march. Our orders were to send those not able to do duty to the Convalescent Camp in Alexandria. The sick are all going to be moved. We are to leave everything not strictly necessary for us to carry to take the fields. So we think there is going to be warm work for us soon. From this Regt. and the 14th there were 450 sent to the Convalescent Camp today. What do you think of that. Our Regt. looks small I tell you. Our company is about as healthy as any and we have only 50 men able to do anything. The other day on battalion drill we had only 18 men. I tell you its whittling them down. Of the Williamstown boys there were only two sent off. [Private] *John Farnham and* [Corporal] *Owin* [Orrin] *Simmons. Both of them had to walk to the station a distance of 4 miles. They were not fit to walk so far but had to. We expect to start tomorrow or next day but cant tell certain. Shall go in a few days. I promise I shall not have a chance to write again very soon. You must write often and I will answer if possible. We are ready for a start. Whatever may be our fate though we hope for an easier task than the one we are performing here. There are so few men for duty that it brings us on guard, picket or patrol almost every night and that is rather tough in stormy weather. We shall probably be held as reserve some where. We take our shelter tents, guns and equipments, 60 rounds of cartridges and seven days rations. Some of the companies cannot raise more than 30 or 35 men. When I spoke of the duty we have been doing I forgot the fatigue. That is shoveling and picking, chopping & etc.*

I received the night before George Stebbin's [George Stebbins died on April 10, 1863, of disease] *death a letter from Gen. A. Simmons informing us that the bounties of twenty five dollars were ready for us. We all wrote our names who we wanted should draw them.*

I went and saw George. He was very sick and we expected that he could not live until morning. He was Perfectly rational. I talked with him about it and he said he wanted I should write to have his mother draw his bounty and I did so. He and the other from our Co. [Private Franklin Slack, of Chelsea, who died on April 6, 1863, of disease] *were buried side by side. They were buried under arms. I tell you it was a solemn day to us here. The beat of the muffled drums, the firing of the salute and above all to know that it was one of our own townsmen and companions. But he is gone and the company mourn his loss for he was a good soldier and an honest boy ever faithful to duty and we all sympathize with his afflicted and mourning parents. But I must hasten to close my letter for it is past bed time now and I was on guard last night in the rain and feel rather old and tired.*

You wanted to know who our Second Lieut. and Orderly was. H. [Horace] *W. Lewis, Esq. of Chelsea formerly our orderly is 2nd Lieut. and Charles Cabot formerly 3rd Sergt. is orderly. He is from the same place* [Chelsea] *and the same as our Capt. The Co. have no voice in the officers. You see the Capt. recommends who he has a mind to be Col. and he sanctions it. They had to have a new corporal and our first Lieut. was from Tunbridge and he wanted one of his men to have it so they put in one of the biggest fools in the Co., but it is military I suppose. The boys perfectly despise our 2nd Lt. H.W.L. and abuse him every way they can. Well I must close. Write soon. Do not worry about me. I am ready to do my duty and meet my fate whatever it may be. If I was to die here I shall and if not I shall return in a few days. So do not for my sake have any fears. I am all right. I should feel bad if I knew you were worrying about me. I am very glad to think I came when I did. I enjoy it first rate most of the time. Give my best respects to all inquiring friends and take a large share for yourselves. Direct as before and I shall get it.*

From your affectionate Son
Henry N. Jillson

After his term of service, Henry returned to Williamstown. In the 1880s or '90s, he moved to Barre, Vermont. On Saturday, April 14, 1900, he was taken to the Waterbury Asylum by Dr. J.W. Jackson. Henry died eleven days later on April 25, 1900. His body was brought back to Williamstown, where he was buried at East Hill Cemetery.[139]

ERASTUS E. MANN

Company D

Erastus Mann, son of Asael and Mary Mann, was born in Wolcott, Vermont, on April 27, 1845. Why he was in Williamstown is something of a mystery, but at age seventeen, he enlisted in Company D, 12th Vermont Infantry Regiment, on August 22, 1862. He was discharged on May 11, 1863, with a disability for partial paralysis of his legs from the effects of typhoid fever. He married Lucy (unknown maiden name). According to the 1870 U.S. census, Erastus and Mary were living in Cady Falls, Vermont. In 1882, Erastus was receiving a two-dollar-a-month government disability pension for the effects of typhoid fever, which he contracted while in the army, and was living in Wolcott, Vermont. Erastus died on December 22, 1923, and was buried at Wolcott's Fairmont Cemetery.[140]

Chester C. Marston

Company D

Chester C. Marston, son of Orvis K. and Caroline Litch Marston, was born in Corinth, Vermont, on January 13, 1844. He enlisted in Company D, 12th Vermont Infantry Regiment, in Williamstown on August 22, 1862. He was mustered out of service on October 4, 1863. After the war, Marston became an attorney and married Jennie S. Bailey on March 16, 1871, in Lisbon, New Hampshire. They settled in Great Falls (present-day Somersworth), New Hampshire, where he drowned in a millpond on April 22, 1874. He was buried at East Thetford Cemetery in East Thetford, Vermont. He left no children.[141]

Oscar F. Marston

Company D

Oscar F. Marston, son of John and Charlotte Wilson Marston, was born in Williamstown on February 9, 1840. According to the 1850 U.S. census, he was not with his parents but was living in Williamstown with Jonathan and Amanda Lewis. In 1860, he was living in the household of a Cynthia Burnham in East Randolph. He enlisted in Company D, 12th Vermont Infantry Regiment, in Williamstown on August 22, 1862. After serving his nine-month obligation, he was mustered out with his regiment on June 14, 1863. Apparently liking military life, and probably enticed by the $600 bounty being paid by Williamstown, he enlisted in the 2nd Vermont Light Artillery the next month, on August 29, 1864 (see p. 141).[142]

Carlos H. Martin

Company D

Carlos H. Martin, son of Dennison and Gratia H. Smith Martin, enlisted in Company D, 12th Vermont Infantry Regiment, in Williamstown on August 22, 1862. He was mustered out of service on July 14, 1863, and returned to Williamstown, but on December 30, 1863, he enlisted in Company C, 8th Vermont Infantry Regiment (see p. 74).[143]

WILLIAM A.S. MCCRILLIS

Company D

William A.S. McCrillis enlisted in Company D, 12th Vermont Infantry Regiment, in Williamstown on August 22, 1862. On January 5, 1863, he was admitted to the regimental hospital for aphonia (inability to speak). He was transferred to Mount Pleasant General Hospital in Washington, D.C., on January 6, and the next day he was transferred to Baxter General in Brattleboro. He regained his voice that summer and was returned to his regiment on July 9. He was mustered out of service on October 4, 1863. After the war, McCrillis lived in Barre for some time before moving to Wolcott, Vermont. He fought with the U.S. Pension Bureau for almost twenty years trying to get a disability pension. Over that time, he claimed he had submitted over 160 affidavits but still was denied a pension. McCrillis died in Wolcott on June 21, 1885, and was buried at Wolcott's Davenport Cemetery.[144]

HENRY H. RECOR

Company D

Henry H. Recor, son of Max and Addle Jellie Recor, both Canadians, was born in Chazey, New York. At some point in time, he moved to Williamstown, where he enlisted in Company D, 12th Vermont Infantry Regiment, in Williamstown on October 22, 1862. After serving his nine months' service, he was mustered out with his regiment on July 14, 1863. After almost a year at home, Recor went back into the army again. Jude Town, of Barre, paid him $300 to be his substitute. The $300 was in addition to large bounties being paid at the time. Recor was assigned to Company A, 5th Vermont, on June 4, 1864 (see p. 49).[145]

BARNEY RING

Company E

Barney Ring, son of Moses and Lucinda Ring, was born in Williamstown. On August 22, 1862, at age twenty-three, he enlisted in Company E, 12th Vermont Infantry Regiment, in Williamstown. He measured five feet, ten inches tall and listed his occupation as a farmer. He had a dark complexion, black eyes and black hair. He was given a disability discharge on November 30, 1862, for typhoid fever, which also caused phthisis (wasting away) of his right testicle. After recovering from his illness, Ring enlisted in Company L, 11th Vermont Infantry Regiment, on June 26, 1863 (see p. 102).[146]

JAMES MARTIN SANFORD

Company D

James M. Sanford was born in New York. He enlisted in Company D, 12th Vermont Infantry Regiment, in Williamstown on August 22, 1862, at age thirty-one. He was mustered out of service on July 14, 1863.[147]

James M. Sanford, Company D, 12th Vermont Infantry Regiment. *Courtesy of Scott Benoir.*

JAMES TEMPLETON SEAVER

Company D

James T. Seaver, son of Cyrus and Lucy Martin Seaver of Williamstown, enlisted in Company D, 12th Vermont Infantry Regiment, in Williamstown on August 22, 1862. He died of typhoid fever at the regimental hospital at Wolf Run Shoals, Virginia, on April 29, 1863. His body was brought back to Vermont and buried at Williamstown's Village Cemetery.[148]

OLNEY FARNHAM SEAVER

Company D

Olney F. Seaver, son of Alvin and Amanda Farnham Seaver, was born in Williamstown on May 24, 1841. He enlisted in Company D, 12th Vermont Infantry Regiment, in Williamstown on August 22, 1862, and listed his occupation as a farmer. He wrote the following letter to his father on July 3, 1863, during the Battle of Gettysburg:

Postwar photograph of Olney F. Seaver, Company D, 12th Vermont Infantry Regiment. *Courtesy of the Williamstown Historical Society.*

Camp at Westminster, Md.
July 3rd 1863

Dear Father

I thought that I would write a few lines to let you know that I am neither killed, wounded or missing. We are here at Westminster about thirty miles from Baltimore in a northwest direction. We started from Wolf Run Shoals a week ago yesterday morning and marched every day till today making eight days march & I tell you we had sore feet when we got here last night about ten o'clock. We started from the Shoals and came through Va. and crossed the Potomac on a pontoon bridge at Edward's Ferry, then went on up to Frederick City and from there to Emittsburg then crossed the line into Penn. And went within three or four miles of Gettysburg where they were having a sharp fight. We stopped there and the rest of the brigade went on to Gettysburg and our regt. came here to guard a supply train that belongs to the first army corps & don't know whether the other regts. will have any part in the fight or not. The fight is still going on and our folks are rather getting the better of them. Today is the third day of the fight. We can hear a constant roar of the cannon but I cannot tell you much on this half sheet. Today is the 3 of July and we have not started for home yet but expect to start from here tomorrow. Some say we shall go to Baltimore tonight but I don't believe we shall get ready to start to tomorrow. There is a rail road runs from this place to Baltimore. I am well only my feet are pretty well blistered and very sore. The boys are well and are glad that we were so lucky as to have a day of rest today. But I cant write any more. So good by

From your son Olney

Seaver was mustered out of service with his regiment on July 14, 1863. After his military service, Olney Seaver returned to Williamstown and resumed farming. He married Marcia Olive Carpenter in Williamstown on December 13, 1866. They had two children: a daughter, Minnie O., who died on November 17, 1874, at age three, and a son named Carl W., who was born on May 27, 1869. Olney died on July 20, 1923, of chronic gastro nephritis (inflammation of the kidneys) and uremia (blood poisoning caused by the kidneys not functioning properly). He was buried at Williamstown's Village Cemetery. Marcia died on July 6, 1933, of carcinoma of the scalp and arteriosclerosis and was buried at Williamstown's Village Cemetery beside her husband.[149]

ORRIN SIMONS

Company D

Orrin Simons, the son of Martin and Orazina Carleton Simons, was born in Williamstown on May 11, 1842. He enlisted in Company D, 12th Vermont Infantry Regiment, in Williamstown on August 22, 1862. He was mustered out of service with his regiment on July 14, 1863. After returning home, Simons enlisted again on December 22, 1863, in Company C, 8th Vermont Infantry Regiment (see p. 76).[150]

GEORGE STEBBINS

Company D

George Stebbins, son of Milo J. and Mehitable Olds Stebbins, was born in Williamstown on January 24, 1844. He enlisted in Company D, 12th Vermont Infantry Regiment, in Williamstown on August 22, 1862. George died of "camp fever" on April 10, 1863, at the regimental hospital at Wolf Run Shoals, Virginia. After George's death, his mother applied for a dependent mother's pension, which she received starting on April 13, 1866, but the six-dollar-a-month pension hardly made up for the loss of her son. Mehitable Stebbins died on June 1, 1900, of a heart attack and was buried at Williamstown's Village Cemetery. There is a stone beside Mehitable with George's name on it. There is no record of his body being shipped back to Williamstown, so it must be a cenotaph.[151]

DANIEL CUSHING TOWNSEND

Company D

Daniel C. Townsend, son of Daniel and Lucreta Snow Townsend, was born on March 13, 1840. He married Francelia "Celia" Flint on August 30, 1863, in Barre, Vermont. Daniel enlisted in Company D, 12th Vermont Infantry Regiment, in Williamstown on August 22, 1862. He contracted typhoid fever while in the army and was given a disability discharge on June 9, 1863. After his discharge from the army, Daniel returned to Williamstown and resumed

Dan Townsend with his Morgan horses. *Courtesy of the Williamstown Historical Society.*

farming. Daniel and Celia had three children: Rosa Lena, born on May 24, 1865; Hector C., born in 1874 and died on February 23, 1876; and Herbert Clarence, born on March 26, 1877. After leaving the army, he received a small disability pension for the loss of his right testicle from suppuration from typhoid fever. Later, he suffered from artery disease, rheumatism, heart problems and a fractured left wrist, and as a result, his pension was increased to fifty dollars a month. Celia died on February 3, 1922, of chronic myocarditis and was buried at Williamstown's Village Cemetery. Daniel died of an intestinal obstruction on June 18, 1923, and was buried beside his wife.[152]

Postwar photograph of Daniel C. and Celia Townsend. Daniel served in Company D, 12th Vermont Infantry Regiment. *Courtesy of the Williamstown Historical Society.*

16
13th VERMONT INFANTRY REGIMENT

The 13th Vermont was mustered in at Brattleboro on October 8, 1862. The 13th Vermont participated in the Battle of Gettysburg, where it lost eleven men killed, eighty-one wounded and twenty-three missing. It was mustered out of service on July 21, 1863.[153]

George W. Blanchard

Company I

George W. Blanchard, son of Hiram and Parthenia Mary Earle Blanchard, was born in Barre, Vermont. He enlisted in Company I, 13th Vermont Infantry Regiment, at age twenty-one in Barre on September 7, 1861, and was selected as a sergeant. The historian of Company I writes of Blanchard:

> *He was a fine musician and the most beautiful singer I ever heard. Every member of the regiment will remember hearing Blanchard, Wood and Gale sing. Many a time the tears trickled down our cheeks when they sang Marion Lee, Zoula Zong, or Rock Me to Sleep, Mother. And many a time when we all had the blues they were dispelled by their witty songs.*

George Blanchard was mustered out on July 21, 1863. He returned to Barre, where he enlisted in Company B, 8th Vermont Infantry Regiment, on December 3, 1863. He mustered out of that regiment on June 28, 1865. He was the brother of Origen A. Blanchard, who served in Company D, 2nd Vermont (see p. 67).[154]

Right: Postwar photograph of George W. Blanchard, Company I, 13th Vermont Infantry Regiment. *Courtesy of the Williamstown Historical Society.*

Orange H. Dickinson

Company E

Orange H. Dickinson enlisted in Company E, 13th Vermont Infantry Regiment, in Cambridge on September 8, 1862. He was mustered out of service with his regiment on July 21, 1863. After returning home, Dickinson enlisted in Company A, 6th Vermont Infantry Regiment, in Cambridge on March 1, 1865, and was mustered out of service on June 26, 1865. Sometime after the war, Orange and his wife, Nancy, moved to Williamstown. Nancy died on April 11, 1897, and she was buried at Williamstown's Village Cemetery. Orange died on December 16, 1904, and was buried beside his wife (see p. 54).[155]

Henry A. Dow

Company I

Henry A. Dow was born in Peacham, Vermont, on February 19, 1843. He enlisted in Company I, 13th Vermont Infantry Regiment, in Barre, Vermont, on August 25, 1862. According to William W. Holden, historian of Company I, 13th Vermont:

Henry Dow, Company I, 13th Vermont Infantry Regiment. *From* History of the 13th Regiment.

Henry A. Dow was a farm laborer and enlisted at Barre, when 19 years old. His comrades remember his peculiar ways and how he used to threaten to scratch our eyes out. *He was second to none in the performance of his duties and was a good soldier.*

He mustered out with his regiment on July 21, 1863. Six months after returning home, Dow enlisted in Company C, 8th Vermont Infantry Regiment, in Williamstown on December 26, 1863 (see p. 68).[156]

GEORGE W. NICHOLS

Company H

Postwar photograph of George W. Nichols, Company H, 13th Vermont Infantry Regiment. *From* History of the 13th Regiment.

George W. Nichols, son of Peter and Hannah Boutwell Nichols, was born on October 27, 1841, in Moretown, Vermont. He enlisted in Company H, 13th Vermont Infantry Regiment, in Barre, Vermont, on August 25, 1862, at age twenty-one. He was mustered out of service on July 21, 1863. After mustering out of the service, he married Hattie A. Davenport of Berlin, daughter of Lyman and Rebecca Reed Davenport, on October 27, 1866. They farmed in Berlin for about five years before settling in Williamstown in 1877. Later in life, George got a twenty-six-dollar-a-month government disability pension for rheumatism. He died on November 21, 1908, of a heart attack and was buried at Williamstown's Village Cemetery. Hattie died of pneumonia on May 27, 1914, at age seventy-three and was buried beside her husband. They had no children.[157]

Charles H. Perry

Company I

Charles H. Perry, son of Heman G. and Betsy Perry, was born on May 13, 1845, in Williamstown. He enlisted in Company I, 13th Vermont Infantry Regiment, in Barre, Vermont, on August 25, 1862. William W. Holden, historian of Company I, 13th Vermont, wrote of Perry:

> *He took kindly to the rough fare of the soldier and pork and beans or hardtack were good enough for him if the quantity was sufficient. He ate so much pork that he was called Pork Perry. He was a good soldier, always*

Charles H. Perry, Company I, 13th Vermont Infantry Regiment. *From* History of the 13th Regiment.

> *doing his duty and after the war he went to Williamstown where he was a good citizen until he died.*

He was mustered out of service with his regiment on July 21, 1863. He enlisted in Company F, 9th Vermont Infantry Regiment, in Orange, Vermont, on January 2, 1864 (see p. 85).[158]

JOSEPH A. SANDERS

Company D

Joseph A. Sanders, son of Henry A. and Martha Lawson Sanders, was born on June 30 in Middlesex, Vermont. He enlisted in Company D, 13th Vermont Infantry Regiment, in Milton, Vermont, on September 6, 1862. In the *History of the 13th Vermont*, the unit historian wrote of Sanders:

> *Joseph Sanders at 21 years of age enlisted in August '62 in Company D at Milton. He was an exceedingly lively young man and even at this writing* [1910], *travels a rapid pace. If there was any frolic in the regiment, or any foraging outside, Sanders was one of the foremost. He did his duty though with much grumbling in hard times. Much inclined to argument, he was always in a wrangle, and added variety, at times when otherwise, it might have been monotonous.*

He was mustered out of service on July 21, 1863. After the war, Sanders returned to Milton but later moved to New York. Then he relocated to Williamstown and became a prosperous farmer. On January 25, 1864, he married Diantha B. Stone, the daughter of Joseph A. and Mary Stone. They had two children: Minnie E. Sanders, born on August 23, 1866, and Perley G. Sanders, born on October 28, 1873. Joseph Sanders died of heart disease on April 23, 1906, and was buried at Williamstown's Village Cemetery. Diantha died of heart disease on November 8, 1920, and was buried beside her husband.[159]

17

14TH VERMONT INFANTRY REGIMENT

The 14th Vermont Infantry Regiment was mustered into service in Brattleboro on October 21, 1862. The 14th Vermont participated in the Battle of Gettysburg, where it lost nineteen men killed, seventy-four wounded and twenty missing. It was mustered out of service on July 30, 1863.

Camp of the 14th Vermont Infantry Regiment at Wolf Run Shoals, Virginia. Photograph by George H. Houghton. *Courtesy of the Vermont Historical Society.*

Samuel B. Rice

Company F

Samuel B. Rice was born in Rutland, Vermont. He enlisted in Company F, 14th Vermont Infantry Regiment, in West Haven, Vermont, on September 3, 1862, at age eighteen. He was slightly wounded on July 3, 1863, at the Battle of Gettysburg. He was mustered out of service on July 30, 1863. He lived in Williamstown for a number of years after the war.[160]

18

15th Vermont Infantry Regiment

The 15th Vermont Infantry Regiment was mustered into service in Brattleboro on October 22, 1862. It was mustered out on August 5, 1863.[161]

Heman G. Perry

Company D

Heman G. Perry was born in Duxbury, Vermont. He married Betsy Abbott in Barre, Vermont, on November 3, 1840. They had eight children: Leander, born on December 10, 1842; Charles H., born on May 13, 1845; Lucy, born on October 2, 1847; John A., born on March 25, 1850; Nancy, born on December 2, 1852; Elizabeth B., born on September 30, 1855; Etta, born on March 20, 1859; and Elmer E., born on August 18, 1861. Heman enlisted in Company D, 15th Vermont Infantry Regiment, in Barre on September 15, 1862, at age forty-three. He came down with typhoid fever on July 16, 1863, and was mustered out of service on August 5, 1863. He made it home but died on September 6, 1863, and was buried at Williamstown's Village Cemetery. After Heman's death, Betsy married Lorenzo D. Smith, who served in the 9th Vermont. He was fifty-three years old, and she was forty-five. Betsy Abbott Perry Smith died in March 1889. Heman Perry's son, Charles H. Perry, served in the 9th and 13th Vermont Infantry Regiments.[162]

FREDRICK BIGELOW STAPLES

Company D

Frederick B. Staples, son of Joseph and Emily Smalley Staples and brother of Charles C. Staples, was born in Williamstown on February 4, 1836. He married Cordelia R. DeGoosh on July 14, 1855, in Randolph. At age twenty-six, he enlisted in Company D, 15th Vermont Infantry Regiment, in Williamstown on September 15, 1862. He was mustered out on August 5, 1863, at the expiration of his service. Frederick Staples died on October 3, 1900, in Bradford, Vermont, and was buried at Bradford's Village Cemetery.[163]

19
17TH VERMONT INFANTRY REGIMENT

Because troops were needed as soon as possible and enlistments were slow, the 17th Vermont Infantry Regiment was mustered into service mostly in squads, when enough men were available. The first detachment was sent south on April 18, 1864; the last arrived on October 27, 1864. The 17th Vermont was brigaded with several regiments from other states in the Ninth Corps. Its first battle was on the second day of the Battle of the Wilderness on May 6, 1864. From there, it participated in the Battles of Spotsylvania, North Anna, Totopotomoy, Bethesda Church and Cold Harbor. The 17th Vermont crossed the James River with the Army of the Potomac and fought at Petersburg. Its most notable battle was at the Crater, where it lost ten men killed, forty-six wounded and eighteen missing. The 17th Vermont participated in the final breakthrough at Petersburg on April 2, 1865, and was mustered out of service on July 14, 1865.[164]

Francis (Frank) F. Parmenter

Company E

Frank F. Parmenter, son of Gilmore and Savina Fisher Parmenter, was born in Williamstown on October 13, 1849. He enlisted in Company E, 17th Vermont Infantry Regiment, in Williamstown on February 17, 1864, and received a $315 town bounty. He told the recruiter that he was eighteen years old and had his father sign his enlistment form giving consent. Frank was, in fact, only fifteen years old when he donned the blue uniform. He was slightly wounded on June 7, 1864, at Cold Harbor, Virginia. On July 30, 1864, during the Battle of the Crater in Petersburg, Virginia, Parmenter was hit in the right shoulder by two Confederate Minié balls. He was admitted to the army hospital at City Point, Virginia, on August 7. He was evacuated to the Cypress Hill General Hospital in Brooklyn, New York, where he died of his wounds on August 21, 1864. He was buried at the Cypress Hill National Cemetery. Frank's father, Gilmore Parmenter, married Savina Fisher in Worcester, Vermont, on February 3, 1835. Savina died in 1858, leaving Gilmore with four young children, one of whom had epilepsy. Gilmore had a bad back from a severe fall, suffered heart trouble and was missing the big toe of his right foot. His toe had been amputated as a result of frostbite. He did light farm chores for his neighbors but earned very little money. Frank had been sending his father part of his army pay to help support the family. After Frank's death, Gilmore applied for a dependent father's pension. He received an $8-a-month government pension starting on August 22, 1864, which was later raised to $12. Gilmore Parmenter died on December 4, 1886.[165]

SAMUEL H. WEBSTER

Company I

Samuel H. Webster, son of Benjamin and Sarah Webster, was born on November 29, 1812, in Roxbury, Vermont. He enlisted in Company I, 17th Vermont Infantry Regiment, in Williamstown on February 10, 1864. He listed his residence as Thetford, Vermont, and his occupation as farmer. He was mustered out on July 14, 1865. He died of peritonitis on February 26, 1875, at age sixty-two and was buried at Williamstown's Village Cemetery.[166]

20
1st Vermont Cavalry Regiment

The 1st Vermont Cavalry Regiment was mustered into service in Burlington on November 19, 1861. On December 26, 1861, it arrived at its camp of instruction in Annapolis, Maryland, where it remained until March 9, 1862, when it left for duty in Virginia's Shenandoah Valley. From that time until the end of the war, the 1st Vermont Cavalry campaigned actively. It participated in sixty-four battles and skirmishes. During its term of service, the 1st Vermont Cavalry lost 63 men killed, 39 who died of wounds and 159 who died in Confederate prisoner of war camps. It was mustered out of service on August 9, 1865.[167]

Joseph O. Gauthier

Company I

Joseph O. Gauthier, son of Magloire and Mary Clair Gauthier, was born in 1844 in St. Gervasia, Canada. He married Melanie Camarair sometime before immigrating to the United States. He enlisted in Company I, 1st Vermont Cavalry Regiment, in Hyde Park, Vermont, on November 4, 1861. He was mustered out of service on November 18, 1864. Sometime after his army service, Gauthier moved to Williamstown, where he worked as a blacksmith. He died in Williamstown on January 10, 1903, of myocarditis and rheumatism and was buried at Williamstown's Village Cemetery. Melanie died of heart disease on May 14, 1904, and was buried beside her husband.[168]

Levi Baxter Richardson

Company C

L. Baxter Richardson was born in 1830 in Marshfield, Vermont. He enlisted in Company C, 1st Vermont Cavalry Regiment, on October 4, 1861. Richardson sustained a hernia and was discharged for a disability on June 1, 1862. He married Emeline Mary White, daughter of Allen and Annie Fisk White of Williamstown. Baxter died in 1872 and was buried at Williamstown's Village Cemetery. Emeline died of a heart attack in Williamstown on April 11, 1923, at age ninety-three and was buried beside her husband.[169]

William F. Ring

Company C

William F. Ring, son of Moses and Lucinda Ring, was born in Williamstown. He enlisted in Company C, 1st Vermont Cavalry Regiment, in Williamstown on October 21, 1861. He was captured on May 24, 1862, at Middletown, Virginia. After his capture, Ring was sent to Richmond, Virginia, where he was imprisoned on Belle Isle for three and a half months. While in confinement, he contracted malaria. He was paroled on September 13, 1862, and returned to his regiment, but because of his malaria, he could no longer hold up as a cavalry trooper and was assigned as a wagon driver on December 29, 1862. In July 1864, at Light House Point, near Prince George Court House, Virginia, he was untying a horse from a picket stake. The horse spooked and spun around, catching Ring's left hand in the halter and breaking his left wrist and damaging the tendons of his fingers. The wrist healed properly, but the fingers were permanently contracted. He was mustered out of service on November 18, 1864. After his military service, Ring applied for and received a government disability pension of four dollars a month commencing on November 18, 1864. After Ring got out of the army, he returned to Williamstown, where he was treated by Dr. Rubilea of Montpelier. In 1879, he was living in Clintonville, New York, where he farmed. By 1910, his disability pension had been increased to twenty-four dollars a month. William Ring died on October 14, 1910, of Bright's disease (kidney disease). He was the brother of Barney Ring.[170]

George Washington Savery (Savory)

Company C

The story of George W. Savery is truly the story of brothers against brothers. George, son of David and Mary Savery, was born in Barre on August 5, 1839, and enlisted in Company C, 1st Vermont Volunteer Cavalry Regiment, in Barre on September 18, 1861. George's brother Jonathan enlisted in the 1st Connecticut Light Artillery. For some reason, two of George's other brothers were in Virginia when war broke out and joined Virginia units. David W. Savery served in both the 18th Battalion, Virginia Heavy Artillery, and E. Graham's Company, Virginia Horse Artillery. Oliver A. Savery served in the 2nd Virginia Infantry, Local Defense, and the 6th Battalion (Tredegar), Virginia Infantry, Local Defense.

George served as a cavalry trooper until he was detailed as a teamster in March 1862. He was sick in the hospital in Winchester, Virginia, from June 19, 1862, until he rejoined his company on August 9, 1862. In February 1863, George was detailed as a teamster for the regimental hospital. He was

Postwar photograph of George W. Savery, Company C, 1st Vermont Cavalry Regiment. *Courtesy of Kristin Hallett.*

mustered out of service on November 19, 1864. George Savery married Flora I. Blanchard, daughter of Chester and Catherine Blanchard, on March 27, 1867, in Barre. Sometime later, they moved to Williamstown, where they bought the old Deacon Abbot farm on West Hill. They had five children: Leslie, Mabel, Mary, Vernon and Willie, who died at age four. Flora died on July 23, 1884, of tuberculosis and was buried at Williamstown's Village Cemetery. On July 9, 1886, George married Fannie Daly, of Plainfield. It was the second marriage for both of them. George sold his farm on West Hill in 1906 and moved to Quarry Street (now Graniteville Road) in Williamstown Village. He was a charter member of Williamstown's Grand Army of the Republic, William Wells Post, No. 113, and was its commander and quartermaster for several years. George died on May 17, 1919, of a heart attack. His funeral was held at the Williamstown Universalist Church on Tuesday, May 20, and he was buried at Williamstown's Village Cemetery.[171]

GILBERT O. SMITH

Company C

Gilbert O. Smith, son of Alvin and Susan Lewis Smith, was born in Northfield, Vermont, on November 13, 1843. He enlisted in Company C, 1st Vermont Cavalry Regiment, in Northfield on September 18, 1861. He was wounded by a Rebel Minié ball in the left elbow joint at the Battle of Gettysburg on July 3, 1863, and was knocked from his horse. The bullet went completely through the elbow joint and put a six-inch split in the humerus. Bone fragments worked their way out of the wound for years. To add insult to injury, Smith was captured after he was wounded, but he escaped a few days later. Smith was transferred to the Veteran Reserve Corps on March 29, 1864, and given a disability discharge on November 16, 1864. After returning from the war, Gilbert moved to Williamstown, where he married Rosina Shephard on October 22, 1867. Gilbert and Rosina had five children: Bertie L., Nettie L., Mary R., Arthur G. and Lila F. By 1897, Smith's arm and fingers were so swollen that he could not dress or undress himself, and he applied for and received a small government disability pension. His pension was eventually increased to forty dollars a month. Gilbert O. Smith died on July 9, 1903, of inflammation of the liver and was buried at Williamstown's Village Cemetery. Rosina died on June 1, 1908, of heart disease and was buried beside her husband.

There is one story worth sharing that involves Gilbert O. Smith. It starts with Daniel F. Skinner, of Chelsea, enlisting in Company H, 4th Vermont Infantry, in Bradford, Vermont, on September 2, 1861. Skinner was mustered in as a sergeant, and on January 9, 1863, he was promoted to first sergeant of Company H. During the second day of the Battle of the Wilderness, Sergeant Skinner was wounded in the thigh by a Rebel Minié ball that shattered his femur. As the Union soldiers were pushed back, Sergeant Skinner was left on the field. That night, his brother, Francis A. Skinner of Chelsea, Vermont, who was also in Company H, went back on the battlefield, found his brother and got him to an aid station. Daniel was finally evacuated back to an army hospital near Fredericksburg, Virginia, where he died of his wound on May 14, 1864. Francis A. Skinner was taken prisoner at the Battle of Weldon Railroad on June 23, 1864, and died of scurvy in Andersonville, Georgia, on August 15, 1864.

Gilbert O. Smith attended the 1892 Grand Army of the Republic National Encampment in Washington, D.C. While riding in a parade through Washington, he struck up a conversation with a Confederate veteran riding along with him. When the Confederate veteran, Rufus B. Merchant, who had been a member of Company A, 9th Georgia Cavalry, found out that Smith was from Vermont, he asked him if, by chance, he knew a Daniel F. Skinner, who had fought in the war. Smith said that he did, and Merchant told him that he had found Skinner's identification tag on the Wilderness battlefield. When Smith returned home, he related the conversation to Daniel and Francis's brother, Austin Skinner of Chelsea. Austin wrote to Merchant and asked if he would return his brother's identification tag, which he did. The identification tag next went to Austin's brother George, who had Daniel's personal effects, diary, tintype and wallet, which had been sent from the hospital where Daniel died. George Skinner married Martha Capron of Williamstown. Martha died at age twenty in 1877 and was buried by her parents at the Williamstown Village Cemetery. Sometime after Martha's death, George moved to Lowell, Massachusetts.[172]

21

COMPANY F, 1ST REGIMENT U.S. SHARPSHOOTERS

The 1st Regiment U.S. Sharpshooters was a very unique unit for its time. It was raised by Colonel Hiram Berdan of New York to consist of long-range snipers. The regiment, most commonly known as Berdan's Sharpshooters, consisted of eight companies from eight different states: Maine, Michigan, Minnesota, New Hampshire, New York, Pennsylvania, Vermont and Wisconsin. To be eligible to enlist in this unique organization, a man had to be able, at public trials, to put ten consecutive shots in a ten-inch-diameter target at two hundred yards. The regiment's uniforms were as distinctive as the men, consisting of green cloth, rather than the usual blue, for camouflage. The men also wore leather leggings and carried knapsacks of tanned leather with the hair still on them. Most took their own rifles when mustered in, but they were soon replaced by government-issued .44-caliber revolving rifles.[173]

Ai Brown

Company F

After mustering out of Company F, 1st Vermont Infantry Regiment, Ai Brown returned to Williamstown and the next month enlisted in Company F, 1st Regiment U.S. Sharpshooters, on September 11, 1861. He was promoted to corporal on December 1, 1862. Brown served with Company F until April 25, 1863, when he deserted from camp near Falmouth, Virginia. He next surfaced, according to the 1870 U.S. census, in Hamburg, Arkansas, where he was farming (see p. 15).[174]

22

2ND VERMONT LIGHT ARTILLERY

The 2nd Vermont Light Artillery was mustered into service in a piecemeal fashion. Six officers and ninety enlisted men were mustered into service on December 16, 1861. Twenty more men were mustered in on December 24, and a final twenty-one were mustered in a little later. The 2nd Vermont Light Artillery went into camp of instruction in Lowell, Massachusetts, the only Vermont unit to rendezvous in another state. It was assigned to General Butler's Division for the capture of New Orleans. The battery landed on Ship Island below New Orleans on March 8, 1862. After the capture, the 2nd Vermont Light Artillery remained in the Deep South and participated in the Battles of Plain's Store, Port Hudson and Jackson, Louisiana. The battery was mustered out of service on July 31, 1865.[175]

CHARLES JAMES CRAM

Charles J. Cram, son of Allen and Catharine Marston Cram, was born in Williamstown on August 28, 1844. He enlisted in the 2nd Vermont Light Artillery in Williamstown on August 19, 1864, and received a $600 town bounty. He was transferred to the 1st Vermont Company Heavy Artillery on March 1, 1865 (see p. 144).[176]

Oscar F. Marston

Oscar F. Marston enlisted in Company D, 12th Vermont Infantry Regiment, in Williamstown on August 22, 1862. After serving his nine-month obligation, he was mustered out with his regiment on June 14, 1863. Apparently liking military life, and probably enticed by a $600 bounty paid by Williamstown, he enlisted in the 2nd Vermont Light Artillery the next month, on August 29, 1864. He was mustered out of service on July 13, 1865. After returning to Williamstown, Oscar married Annett "Nettie" Webster on June 30, 1869. In the 1870 U.S. census, they were living in Concord, New Hampshire, with Horace and Mary Beal. In the 1910 U.S. census, Nettie was a widow living in Lawrence, Massachusetts (see p. 115).[177]

23
3RD VERMONT LIGHT ARTILLERY

Recruiting for the 3rd Vermont Light Artillery commenced in August 1863. Because the regiments of the Second Vermont Brigade mustered out in July, it was thought that recruitment would go quickly for the battery. However, veterans of the Second Vermont Brigade were reluctant to reenlist, and the 3rd Vermont Light Artillery was not filled until December 1863. The battery was mustered into service in Burlington on January 1, 1864, and headed south on January 15. After reaching Washington, D.C., on January 18, the battery marched to Camp Barry, the artillery camp of instruction, on the Bladensburg Road. Here, the battery received its horses and guns, and the men trained to be artillerymen. On April 29, the battery was assigned to the Ninth Corps and received orders to march south to join the Army of the Potomac. It reached the army in time to join in Grant's Overland Campaign, starting on May 5, but did not actively participate in any of the battles until it reached Petersburg. At Petersburg, the 3rd Vermont Light Artillery fought in the Battles of the Crater, Globe Tavern, Fort Stedman and the final breakthrough on April 2, 1865. The 3rd Vermont was mustered out of service on June 13, 1865.[178]

Henry H. Boutwell

Henry H. Boutwell enlisted in Company B, 6th Vermont Infantry Regiment, in Williamstown on October 3, 1861. He was mustered out of service on

September 1862 with a disability discharge due to illness. After returning to Williamstown, Boutwell married Philinda Mason on October 11, 1863. After recovering from the illness he had contracted in the army, Henry enlisted in the 3rd Vermont Light Artillery on August 29, 1864, and received a $600 town bounty. He served without incident and was mustered out of service on June 15, 1865. Henry Boutwell died of dropsy (a swelling of all, or a part, of the body) on November 17, 1881, and was buried at Williamstown's Village Cemetery (see p. 53).[179]

Joseph Mason

Joseph Mason enlisted in the 3rd Vermont Light Artillery in Williamstown on August 16, 1864, and received a $600 bounty. He was mustered out at the expiration of service on June 15, 1865.[180]

24
1ST VERMONT COMPANY HEAVY ARTILLERY

Because the 2nd Vermont Light Artillery had received so many recruits by March 1865, 119 men were reassigned to a newly formed unit named the 1st Vermont Company of Heavy Artillery for service in the fortifications at Port Hudson, Louisiana. The company was mustered out of service on July 28, 1865.[181]

CHARLES JAMES CRAM

Charles J. Cram, son of Allen and Catherine Marston Cram, enlisted in the 2nd Vermont Light Artillery in Williamstown on August 19, 1864, and received a $600 town bounty. He was transferred to the 1st Vermont Company Heavy Artillery on March 1, 1865. He was mustered out of service on July 28, 1865. Cram married Mary J. Evans, daughter of Arnold L. and Clarissa Libby Evans of Northfield, on March 7, 1866, in Montpelier. They had two children: Etta M., born on October 14, 1866, and Mattie E., born on August 10, 1876. Mary died of diabetes at age sixty-nine on January 21, 1917, and was buried at Williamstown's Village Cemetery. Charles J. Cram died of a cerebral embolism and chronic internal nephritis on February 11, 1921, at age seventy-six and was buried beside his wife. At the time of his death, he was receiving a $50-a-month government disability pension for malaria, which he contracted in the army (see p. 140).[182]

25
VETERAN RESERVE CORPS

The Veteran Reserve Corps was established in the Union army in April 1863 as the Invalid Corps. It consisted of officers and men with wounds or illnesses that would not allow them to serve in the field but would let them continue to serve doing light duty away from the front, such as guard duty at military hospitals, nurses, clerks, warehousemen, etc. By December 1863, there were over twenty thousand men in its ranks. Because "Invalid Corps" was considered by the soldiers to be a derogatory term, the name was changed to the Veteran Reserve Corps in March 1864.[183]

Jason Johnson

Jason Johnson enlisted in Company B, 4th Vermont Infantry Regiment, on August 22, 1862, and was mustered out of service on September 30, 1864. He enlisted in Company D, 1st Regiment, of the Veteran Reserve Corps in Johnson, Vermont, on January 23, 1865. He was mustered out of service on January 22, 1866. A short time after leaving the army, Johnson moved to Williamstown, where he farmed. He married Julia Merrill, daughter of Hezihial and Nancy Horn Merrill. He was very active in Williamstown's William Wells Post, No. 113, of the Grand Army of the Republic. In January 1898, Jason Johnson had a very close call. As he was descending the hill just above his house, the king bolt broke and let his carriage drop to the ground. Johnson was thrown beneath the horse's feet but hung on to the reins and came out all right, except for a thorough shaking up. Years later, on May 21, 1922, Jason Johnson died of stomach and liver cancer in Williamstown and was buried at Williamstown's Village Cemetery. After Jason's death, Julia Johnson moved in with her daughter, Mrs. Fred Currier, in Richmond, Vermont, where she died of heart disease on April 22, 1923. Her body was brought back to Williamstown to be buried beside her husband (see p. 39).[184]

26
UNASSIGNED RECRUITS

Patrick Branagan

Patrick Branagan enlisted in Williamstown on September 1, 1864, and received a $600 bounty from the town. He was shipped to the recruit collection camp in New Haven, Connecticut, and on October 11, 1864, he was discharged, probably for some health reason. Whether he got to keep his bounty is unknown.[185]

Frank Edward Cross

Frank E. Cross, son of Francis and Eliza Cross, was born in Colchester, Vermont, about 1858. He enlisted in the army in Colchester on January 5, 1865. He was mustered into service that same day and was sent to the recruit collection camp in New Haven, Connecticut. On January 26, 1865, he was discharged, probably for some health reason. Sometime after the war, Frank Cross moved to Williamstown, where he worked as a carpenter. He died of tuberculosis on September 1, 1900, and was buried at Williamstown's Village Cemetery.[186]

27
U.S. ARMY REGULAR OFFICERS

FREDERICK MARCY LYNDE

Frederick M. Lynde, son of Isaac Lynde and Margaret Wight Lynde, was born on September 10, 1843, in Fiske, Wisconsin, where his father was stationed in the army. He returned to Williamstown and enlisted in Company B, 4th Vermont Infantry Regiment, on August 20, 1861. Soon after enlisting, he was selected as a sergeant. He was promoted to second lieutenant on May 15, 1862, but resigned his commission on July 31, 1862. He later enlisted as a private in Company C, 1st Wisconsin Heavy Artillery, on August 18, 1863. In that unit, he was promoted to sergeant on February 17, 1865. He was mustered out of service on September 23, 1865.

Following in the footsteps of his father, Frederick Lynde was commissioned in the regular army as a second lieutenant in the 22nd U.S. Infantry Regiment on July 28, 1866. He married Williamanna Elzy in 1868 in Baltimore, Maryland. He was promoted to first lieutenant in February 1869. For some reason, he was unassigned from May 15, 1869, until December 31, 1870, when he was assigned to the 1st U.S. Infantry Regiment. He was promoted to captain on September 20, 1883. Due to a number of illnesses, Lynde was retired on a disability on September 20, 1883. He died on December 26, 1898.

After Franklin's death, Williamanna Lynde received a seventeen-dollar-a-month government pension and moved to Picolata, Florida, where she lived with her father-in-law, Major Isaac Lynde. By 1902, the sixty-six-year-old Williamanna was in extremely poor health. She suffered from erysipelas (an acute skin disease caused by a species of streptococcus and marked by localized inflammation and fever; it is quite painful), neuralgia and lung problems. Her condition required constant care and medical attention, and her income, aside from her seventeen-dollar-a-month government pension, was less than ninety dollars a year. Additionally, she was unable to do manual labor to support herself. For those reasons, her pension was raised to thirty dollars a month (see p. 42).[187]

Isaac Lynde

One of the most egregious breaches of military justice during the Civil War happened to Major Isaac Lynde. His story will be told in four phases. The first phase concerns Isaac himself. Isaac Lynde, son of Cornelius and Rebekah Davis Lynde, was born in Williamstown on July 23, 1804. He had the good fortune of being born into a very prominent family. His father, a Harvard graduate, was one of the original proprietors of Williamstown and one of the first five men to settle the town. His mother, Rebekah, was the daughter of Colonel Jacob Davis, a pioneer and developer of Montpelier.

Postwar photograph of Isaac Lynde, 7th U.S. Infantry Regiment. *Courtesy of the Williamstown Historical Society.*

Isaac was the eighth of Cornelius and Rebekah Lynde's ten children. He graduated from the U.S. Military Academy at West Point, New York, in 1827 and was commissioned a second lieutenant in the 5th U.S. Infantry. That fall, on September 18, 1827, he married Margaret Wight in Williamstown. They were married in the Williamstown Congregational Church by Reverend Joel Davis. Margaret was the daughter of

Margaret Lynde, wife of Isaac Lynde. *Courtesy of the Williamstown Historical Society.*

Williamstown residents Simeon and Esther Smith Wight.

Shortly after their wedding, the Lyndes set off on Isaac's military career. Isaac remained with the 5th U.S. Infantry for many years, being promoted to first lieutenant on February 18, 1836, and to captain on January 1, 1839. He served in the Mexican War and was promoted to major on October 18, 1855.

The firing on Fort Sumter on April 12, 1861, by Confederate forces signaled the outbreak of the Civil War. At that time, Major Lynde was in command of the U.S. 7th Infantry at Fort Lane, New Mexico. During that time, many Union officers were resigning their commissions and joining the Confederate army. Some had to surrender their commands because they suddenly found themselves in enemy territory; this was especially true in the Southwest. On June 23, Major Lynde was ordered to move his command to Fort Filmore, New Mexico, to consolidate with several other units. Lynde and his command arrived at Fort Filmore on July 4, 1861.

Fearing attack by Union forces, Confederate lieutenant colonel John R. Baylor, with a battalion of 250 men from the 2nd Texas Mounted Rifles, left Fort Bliss, Texas, during the night of July 23 to attack Fort Filmore. Detecting the approach of the Rebel troops, Lynde led a force of 380 men a few miles from Fort Filmore to the town of Mesilla. Here, Lynde's force met Baylor's. Lynde demanded that Baylor surrender, but Baylor refused. Lynde then deployed his men and opened up on the Rebels with his artillery. The infantry was ordered to advance, but heavy sand and cornfields, in which they were fighting, interfered with the advance. Next, Lynde ordered his cavalry to charge Baylor's men. The cavalry charge was met by a hail of bullets and was quickly broken up. Lynde then re-formed his command and pulled back to Fort Filmore. Although reports differ, Lynde lost somewhere between 3 and 13 men killed and 2 officers and 4 men wounded, while Baylor lost 2 dead and 7 seriously wounded.

On the morning of July 26, Major Lynde decided he could not defend Fort Filmore and would take his command to the safety of Fort Stanton. After destroying all the government supplies that they could not take with them, the command departed. In addition to his 540-some soldiers, Lynde also had a large contingent of wives and laundry women. The route chosen would take the column through the San Augustine Pass to St. Augustine Spring some twenty-five miles from Fort Filmore, where they could water their animals and fill their canteens.

After daybreak, the July heat—which was soon over one hundred degrees—started taking its toll on the infantry providing the rear guard, and many men fell out of the ranks. Before long, Colonel Baylor's cavalrymen started scooping up the straggling Federal infantrymen. As Lynde and the head of the column reached the spring, Baylor and his men were on high ground staring down at them. With his ranks depleted, and considering the safety of the women, Lynde surrendered to the Confederates. Not wanting to be strapped with all the Union prisoners, Baylor paroled them, and they eventually made their way to Jefferson Barracks, Missouri.

By the time Lynde made it to Jefferson Barracks, he had already been dismissed from the army on November 25, 1861. Lynde tried to get a hearing or court-martial to clear his name, but to no avail. He went to Washington to try to talk to the president, but Lincoln would not see him. The Lincoln administration had its scapegoat, and that was it. Lynde's thirty-seven years of honorable service to his country were for naught.

Phase two of this story overlaps phase one. It starts with Fredrick Tracy Dent and Ulysses S. Grant graduating together from West Point in the class of 1843. The two young second lieutenants were stationed together at Jefferson Barracks, near the Dent family home in St. Louis. It was here that U.S. Grant met Frederick's sister, Julia, who became Mrs. Grant on August 22, 1848, just before he left for the Mexican War. Frederick Dent also served in the Mexican War, where he received two brevet promotions for gallant and meritorious conduct in combat. During the action for which he received his second brevet, he was severely wounded but survived. After the war, he married Helen Louise Lynde, Major Isaac Lynde's daughter, on August 3, 1853. At the outbreak of the Civil War, Dent was a captain serving in San Francisco, California, where he remained until 1863. At that time, he was promoted to major and assigned to New York City. In the spring of 1864,

Frederick T. Dent, U.S. Army. *Courtesy of the U.S. Army Military History Institute.*

Louise Lynde Dent, wife of Frederick T. Dent. *Courtesy of the Williamstown Historical Society.*

Lieutenant General U.S. Grant appointed Dent as his aide-de-camp, and by the end of the war he was a brevet brigadier general. After the war, Dent served as Grant's military secretary.

The third phase of Isaac Lynde's story is his redemption. It was probably just after the war that Dent and Grant lobbied the War Department to reinstate Major Lynde to active duty and clear his record. On November 27, 1866, after being pilloried by the Lincoln administration, President Andrew Johnson reinstated Isaac Lynde as a major in the 18th U.S. Infantry and then retired him the same day. Sometime just before, or just after, his reinstatement, Isaac Lynde moved to Picolata, Florida, near St. Augustine, where he piloted a tugboat. He died on April 13, 1886, and was buried in Baltimore, Maryland.

The fourth and final phase of Isaac Lynde's story happened 123 years after his death. After years of research and fascination with the Isaac Lynde story, Gerald Hinckley, a 30-year resident of Williamstown, discovered that Lynde's biography published in the West Point *Register of Graduates* states that Major Isaac Lynde surrendered his force "to an inferior force of insurgents." Incensed, Hinckley wrote to Vermont senator Patrick Leahy on June 20, 2009, with the facts of the Lynde case and asked him to help clear Lynde's name in the West Point register. Leahy's office forwarded Hinckley's letter to the U.S. Military Academy. Hinckley received a letter from the chief of staff of West Point on August 10, 2009, informing him that they had looked into the matter and had contacted the West Point Association of Graduates, which publishes the *Register of Graduates*. As a result, the association agreed to change the wording in Lynde's biography. The next issue of the register, which was published in 2010, had the wording changed from "surrendered his command at Fort Filmore, New Mexico, on July 27, 1861, to an inferior force of insurgents" to a new version: "surrendered his command at Fort Filmore, New Mexico, on July 27, 1861, to invading Confederate forces."[188]

George Wilkins Smith

George W. Smith, son of Ira and Lavinia Clark Smith, was born in Williamstown, Vermont, on April 4, 1840. While Smith was still a boy, his family moved to Lebanon, New Hampshire, where he attended the public schools and prepared for college at Kimball Union Academy in Meriden, New Hampshire. He entered Norwich University but left in 1862 to enlist in the army. Smith enlisted in Company E, 17th U.S. Infantry, on May 10, 1862. He was promoted to corporal and then to sergeant. He was commissioned as a second lieutenant on October 13, 1862, and as a first lieutenant on December 11, 1862. Smith commanded his company in the Second Battle of Bull Run and at Antietam and Fredericksburg. He served as regimental quartermaster of the 17th Infantry from June 15, 1864, to October 19, 1865, when he was promoted to captain. He was transferred to the 35th U.S. Infantry on September 21, 1866.

After the close of the war, Smith was transferred to the Department of Texas. He resigned his commission on December 31, 1869, and returned north. In 1870, he returned to Texas and was commissioned as a colonel in the Texas State Militia. He took an active part in the reconstruction work in Texas and in the establishment of the first public schools in that state. In 1873, Smith resigned his position and returned north, settling in Philadelphia, Pennsylvania, where he was employed by James W. Cooper, a

George Wilkins Smith, U.S. Army. *From* Norwich University, 1819–1911.

furniture manufacturer. In 1878, he started his own furniture manufacturing firm named George W. Smith & Co. On June 16, 1870, George W. Smith married Nellie Frances Dearborn of Exeter, New Hampshire. They had three children: Arthur Dearborn, born on March 11, 1871; George Sydney, born on January 17, 1873; and Rayburn Clark, born on July 7,1877. George W. Smith died in Philadelphia on October 13, 1896.[189]

28
WILLIAMSTOWN MEN WHO SERVED IN OTHER STATE UNITS

James Edward Ainsworth

Company F, 12th Iowa Infantry Regiment

James Edward Ainsworth, son of Ralph Ainsworth and Polly D. Chase Ainsworth, was born in Claremont, New Hampshire, on June 3, 1830. He attended the public schools in Claremont and then entered Kimball Union Academy in Meriden, New Hampshire. Ainsworth graduated from the University of New Hampshire in 1853. In the fall of 1854, he moved to Dubuque, Iowa, where he worked as a civil engineer for a railroad company. In the fall of 1861, he enlisted in Company F, 12th Iowa Infantry Regiment, and was commissioned as its captain on November 12, 1861. Being unable to endure the exposure and privations of army life, Ainsworth resigned his commission soon after the Battle of Shiloh on April 19, 1862, and returned to engineering. On December 19, 1867, he married his cousin, Laura L. Ainsworth of Williamstown. She was the daughter of Calvin Ainsworth and Laura Lynde Ainsworth. They had no children.

Ainsworth, the county seat of Brown County, Nebraska, was named for J. Edward Ainsworth, who surveyed the area and helped bring the railroad there. In 1893, he retired from active engineering work and moved to Moline, Illinois. In the late 1890s, Edward and Laura moved to Williamstown. J. Edward Ainsworth died on August 30, 1907, of heart disease and was buried at Williamstown's Village Cemetery. Laura Ainsworth died on April 6, 1925, of arteriosclerosis and was buried beside her husband.[190]

Postwar photograph of James Edward Ainsworth, Company F, 12th Iowa Infantry Regiment. *Courtesy of the Williamstown Historical Society.*

Laura Ainsworth, wife of James Edward Ainsworth. *Courtesy of the Williamstown Historical Society.*

Andrew Whitmore Beckett

Company B, 113th Illinois Infantry Regiment

Andrew W. Beckett, son of William S. Beckett and Polly Poole Beckett, was born in Williamstown on June 4, 1831. He was a tall, handsome man with blue eyes and brown hair. He left Williamstown in 1849 to travel west. He married Sarah Adeline Germaine in Rock Island, Illinois, on August 5, 1856. They settled in Martinton, Illinois, where Andrew was a lawyer. He enlisted in Company B, 113th Illinois Infantry Regiment, on August 7, 1862. He was commissioned as first lieutenant of Company B on October 1, 1862, and as captain of Company B on August 26, 1863. Andrew suffered a great deal with chronic diarrhea and was at home on furlough a good deal of the time. He was given a disability discharge from the army on June 20, 1865. His army service had taken quite a toll on Andrew, and he died on February 27, 1869, of chronic diarrhea. After his death, Sarah received a veteran widow's pension from the government. Sadly, Sarah died on July 8, 1874, leaving five children—George W., Mary E., Francis E., Emily A. and Merrill P.—orphans. The children were raised under the guardianship of a Mr. Thaddeus Wade. The Beckett children each received a seventeen-dollar-a-month pension from the government until they were sixteen years old.[191]

Andrew W. Beckett, Company B, 113th Illinois Infantry Regiment. *Courtesy of the Williamstown Historical Society.*

Isaac L. Clark, 96th Illinois Infantry Regiment. *Courtesy of the Roger D. Hunt Collection at the U.S. Army Military History Institute.*

ISAAC L. CLARK

96th Illinois Infantry Regiment

Isaac L. Clark was born in Williamstown in 1824 and graduated from Dartmouth College in July 1848. He married Philinda Willey of Grafton, Vermont, and a year after his graduation they moved to Waukegan, Illinois, where he was the principal of the academy there. In May 1853, he was admitted to the bar and soon had a lucrative practice. Isaac and Philinda had only one child, a son they named Elam L. Clark. Isaac was commissioned captain of Company G, 96th Illinois Infantry Regiment, on July 22, 1862. He was promoted to lieutenant colonel of the regiment on September 6, 1862. Isaac was killed in action on September 20, 1863, at the Battle of Chickamauga. After Isaac's death, Philinda and Elam returned to Grafton, Vermont.[192]

JOHN COUGHLIN

10th New Hampshire Infantry Regiment

John Coughlin was born in Williamstown. When the Civil War broke out, he was twenty-five years old and was living in Manchester, New Hampshire. He was commissioned as lieutenant colonel of the 10th New Hampshire Infantry Regiment on September 5, 1862. Coughlin was wounded twice during the war—once at Port Walthall, on May 7, 1864, near Petersburg and again on July 30, 1864, at the Battle of the Crater. He was promoted to brevet colonel and then to brevet brigadier general of U.S. Volunteers on April 9, 1865, for gallant conduct in the field. He was mustered out of service on June 21, 1865. Coughlin was awarded the Medal of Honor on August 24, 1893, for gallant and meritorious service during a sudden night attack at Swift's Creek, Virginia, on May 9, 1864, against Burnham's Brigade, which was thrown into confusion. Without waiting for orders, Lieutenant Colonel Coughlin led his regiment forward and positioned it between the advancing enemy and Union artillery, thus saving the guns. After the war, he lived in Washington, D.C. He is buried at Arlington National Cemetery.[193]

John Coughlin, 10th New Hampshire Infantry Regiment. *Courtesy of the Roger D. Hunt Collection at the U.S. Army Military History Institute.*

John Lynde Jr.

Company D, 2nd Iowa Infantry Regiment

John Lynde Jr., son of John Lynde and Dolly Smith Lynde, was born in Williamstown on February 21, 1835. In the fall of 1856, he moved to Will County, Illinois, where he taught school and studied law. He was admitted to the bar in Polk County, Iowa. He enlisted in Company D, 2nd Iowa Infantry Regiment, as a private on May 27, 1861, at age twenty-five. He was promoted to corporal on July 16, 1861, and to quartermaster sergeant on March 4, 1862. He was commissioned a second lieutenant in Company D on June 23, 1862. John Lynde Jr. resigned from the army on May 23, 1864,

John Lynde Jr., Company D, 2nd Iowa Infantry Regiment. *Courtesy of the Williamstown Historical Society.*

at the expiration of his service. In 1866, he worked as a civilian employee in the U.S. Army Quartermaster's Department. In 1870, he was appointed as a clerk in the U.S. Postal Department in Washington, D.C. As the years went on, John's health slowly declined, and he received a military disability pension for heart trouble and bronchitis. In May 1877, Lynde returned to Williamstown, where he died on March 31, 1912, of chronic nephritis and was buried at Williamstown's Village Cemetery.[194]

JOSEPH B. NORRIS

Company F, 16th, and Company A, 121st New York Infantry Regiments

Joseph B. Norris, son of Jesse and Sovina C. Norris, was born in Peru, New York. He initially enlisted in Company F, 16th New York Infantry Regiment, but was transferred to Company A, 121st New York Infantry Regiment, on May 12, 1863. He was wounded twice at the Battle of Cedar Creek, Virginia, on October 19, 1864. First, a Rebel Minié ball hit him on the inside of his right calf about three inches below his knee, passing completely through. Then, a shell fragment struck him in the back. The shell wound, while painful, did not do much damage. The leg wound, however, kept him in army hospitals until he received a disability discharge on June 12, 1865. He had to use crutches for some time after his discharge. After the war, he settled in Williamstown, where he farmed. On June 14, 1869, Joseph married Emaline Stave in Peru, New York. Joseph died of asthma and heart disease on April 27, 1884, at age sixty-two and was buried at Williamstown's East Hill Cemetery. Emaline applied for a veteran widow's pension after Joseph's death but was turned down.[195]

Joseph B. Norris, Company F, 16th, and Company A, 121st New York Infantry Regiments, displaying his wound to the U.S. Pension Bureau. *Courtesy of the National Archives.*

John S. Poor

2nd Company New Hampshire Heavy Artillery

John S. Poor was born in Williamstown. At age eighteen, he enlisted in the 2nd Company New Hampshire Heavy Artillery in Goffstown, New Hampshire, on August 27, 1863. His unit was assigned to the fortifications that surrounded the nation's capital. Poor deserted from Fort Foote, Maryland, on August 23, 1864. His last known residence after the war was in Somerville, Massachusetts.[196]

GEORGE F. TAPLIN

Company E, 12th New Hampshire Infantry Regiment

George F. Taplin was born in Williamstown. He enlisted in Company E, 12th New Hampshire Infantry Regiment, on November 3, 1863. At that time, he was an eighteen-year-old boy who stood five feet, eight inches tall and had blue eyes. He listed his occupation as a student. Somehow Taplin was inducted into the army, even though he suffered from epilepsy, and was never discharged, even though he would continue to have seizures. Taplin was shot in the left thigh on June 3, 1864, at the Battle of Cold Harbor, Virginia. The shot shattered his femur, and he spent the rest of his military career in army hospitals until he was given a disability discharge on April 18, 1865. By 1870, he was living in Canaan, New Hampshire, and was receiving a twenty-five-dollar-a-month government pension for his wound. George Taplin died on December 22, 1870, in Bradford, Vermont.[197]

GEORGE H. WATSON

Company C, 2nd, and Company B, 17th New Hampshire Infantry Regiments

George H. Watson enlisted in Company C, 2nd New Hampshire Infantry Regiment, on September 25, 1862, at age forty. He was transferred to Company B, 17th New Hampshire Infantry Regiment, on November 7, 1862. Watson was detailed to the regimental band on April 10, 1863. After the war, Watson moved to Williamstown, where he died on February 24, 1880. He was buried at Williamstown's Village Cemetery.[198]

29
U.S. NAVY

William C. Chapman

William C. Chapman enlisted in the U.S. Navy in 1865. He served aboard the USS *Kearsarge*, USS *Tahoma* and USS *Saratoga*. He was discharged on February 13, 1868.[199]

Patrick Hennessy

Patrick Hennessy enlisted in the U.S. Navy in February 1865. He served on the steam sloops of war USS *Wachusett* and USS *Hartford*. He was discharged on August 14, 1868.[200]

Albert Pulsifier

Albert Pulsifier enlisted in the U.S. Navy in February 1865. He served aboard the USS *Marblehead*, USS *Marion*, USS *Tonawanda* and USS *Santee*. He was discharged on February 27, 1868.[201]

30

WILLIAMSTOWN'S LAST TWO CIVIL WAR VETERANS

Charles I. Preston and Peter La Belle

By 1931, there were only two Civil War veterans left living in Williamstown: Charles I. Preston and Peter La Belle. On Wednesday, June 24, Preston, age eighty-three, died at 1:00 a.m. of pneumonia. The son of Benjamin and Nancy Preston, he was born in Cabot on February 22, 1848. On August 25, 1864, at age sixteen (although he said he was eighteen), he enlisted in Company G, 2nd Vermont Infantry Regiment, in Underhill, Vermont. Interestingly, his four brothers also enlisted in the army. George W. Preston enlisted in Company K, 8th Vermont; Thomas H. Preston enlisted in Company L, 1st Vermont Cavalry; John Preston enlisted in Company G, 4th Vermont; and Solon H. Preston enlisted in Company H, 11th Vermont. All five of the Preston boys survived the war without a scratch. Charles was mustered out of service on June 19, 1865.

After the war, Preston lived in Marshfield. In the 1920s, he moved to Williamstown and worked as a carpenter and builder. Preston was very active in the Williamstown Grand Army of the Republic, William Wells Post, No. 113. He was survived by his brother Solon H. Preston, eighty-six, of Burlington; one son, Ellis C. Preston of Burlington; two daughters, Mrs. George Smith of Marshfield and Miss Marcia Preston of New York; a stepdaughter, Mrs. Orrin Shepardson of Foxboro, Massachusetts; six grandchildren; and two great-grandchildren. Charles Preston's funeral was held in Williamstown on Friday, June 26, at the home of Katie

Hadlock, where he lived. He was buried at the Durant Cemetery in Lower Cabot, Vermont.

Upon hearing of his comrade's death, Peter La Belle, age ninety, now Williamstown's last living Civil War veteran, made arrangements to attend his GAR comrade's funeral, but he unexpectedly died at 5:30 a.m. on Thursday, June 25, of prostatitis and cystitis. He died on the farm of his son, Arthur La Belle, in Williamstown.

Peter La Belle, the son of Lewis and Julia Sweeny, was born on July 15, 1840, in Burlington. His father was a French immigrant, and his mother was born in Three Rivers, Canada. Peter enlisted in Company E, 1st Vermont Cavalry Regiment, in Williston on December 15, 1863. He was mustered out on August 9, 1865.

After returning from the army, Peter married Laura LaBounty of Essex Junction on October 3, 1865. They resided in Essex Junction until 1899, when they moved to Williamstown. He had been active up to the time of his death. In fact, two weeks prior to his death he was in Montreal on a fishing trip with his family. He worked on his son's farm in the summers and wintered with his daughter, Mrs. A.E. Derschers, in Montreal. Peter's death came as a great shock to his wife, Julia, who had been his constant companion during sixty-five years of marriage. He also left one other daughter, Mrs. Frank Wheaton of Montpelier, and several grandchildren and great-grandchildren.

La Belle's funeral was held at the Church of the Holy Family in Essex Junction at 10:00 a.m. on June 26, and he was buried at the family lot in Essex Junction. Within an hour or two of La Belle's funeral, his Grand Army of the Republic comrade Charles I. Preston, whose funeral La Belle had planned to attend, was also laid to rest.[202]

NOTES

Chapter 1

1. Williamstown Historical Society, *History of Williamstown*, 21–22; Town Record, Book No. 4, Town Clerk's Office, Williamstown, VT, pp. 150–58.

Chapter 2

2. Benedict, *Vermont in the Civil War*, vol. 1, 28–61.
3. Peck, *Revised Roster*, 19, 601; Martin Family Papers; Benedict, *Vermont in the Civil War*, vol. 2, 731–33.
4. Peck, *Revised Roster*, 19; "Cemetery Database," Vermont in the Civil War, http://vermontcivilwar.org/cem/cemetery.php; Charles E. Davis, compiled military service record, Records of the Adjutant General's Office, 1780–1917, Record Group 94, National Archives Building, Washington, D.C. (hereafter cited as the individual's name, type of record).
5. Peck, *Revised Roster*, 19; Works Progress Administration Veteran Grave Index, Vermont Historical Society, Barre, VT (hereafter cited as WPA Grave Index).
6. Peck, *Revised Roster*, 16; Child, *Gazetteer of Orange County*, 518.

Chapter 3

7. Boatner, *Civil War Dictionary*, 869–70; Benedict, *Vermont in the Civil War*, 131, 240–620.

CHAPTER 4

8. Benedict, *Vermont in the Civil War*, vol. 1, 62–125.
9. Peck, *Revised Roster*, 44; Cemetery Book and Vital Records (Death), Book No. 7, Town Clerk's Office, Williamstown, VT, p. 4; Ancestry.com, www.ancestry.com; Origen A. Blanchard's compiled military service and military pension records.
10. Peck, *Revised Roster*, 54; John E. Clough, compiled military service; John E. Clough, military pension record; *Montpelier Argus and Patriot*, June 20, 1924.
11. Peck, *Revised Roster*, 51; Thomas Clury, compiled military service record.
12. Peck, *Revised Roster*, 51; Ralph Ditty, military pension record; Child, *Gazetteer of Orange County*, 524.
13. Peck, *Revised Roster*, 51.
14. Ibid., 52; *Williamstown Herald*, June 17, 1898; Francis S. Martin, military pension record; Dr. Henry L. Janes's Medical Journal, Special Collections, Bailey/Howe Library, University of Vermont, Burlington, VT, p. 369; Zeller, *Second Vermont*, 228–29; Vital Records, Book 1B (Death), Town Clerk's Office, Williamstown, VT, p. 9; *Walton's Journal*, October 13, 1865.
15. Peck, *Revised Roster*, 52; Vital Records, Book 6 (Death), and Book 8 (Death), Town Clerk's Office, Williamstown, VT, pp. 13, 76; Child, *Gazetteer of Orange County*, 523; Joseph A. Sander, military pension record.
16. Peck, *Revised Roster*, 43; Vital Records, Cemetery Book, Town Clerk's Office, Williamstown, VT; Eldon A. Tilden, compiled military service and military pension records.
17. Peck, *Revised Roster*, 50, 314; Charles A. White, compiled military service and military pension records.

CHAPTER 5

18. Benedict, *Vermont in the Civil War*, vol. 1, 126–53.
19. Peck, *Revised Roster*, 87; Martin Family Papers; Williamstown Historical Society, *History of Williamstown*, 58; John W. Bacon, military pension record; *Montpelier Argus and Patriot*, June 13, 1900; Hemenway, *Vermont Historical Gazetteer*, vol. 2, 1148.
20. Peck, *Revised Roster*, 103; *Montpelier Argus and Patriot*, February 9, 1897; William H. Hamilton, compiled military service record.
21. Peck, *Revised Roster*, 101; Vermont Vital Records (microfilm), Vermont Historical Society, Barre, VT (hereafter cited as Vermont Vital Records); WPA Grave Index; Ancestry.com, www.ancestry.com; Alden Slack, compiled military service and military pension records.

CHAPTER 6

22. Benedict, *Vermont in the Civil War*, 156–77.
23. Peck, *Revised Roster*, 115; Martin Family Papers; Vermont Vital Records; "Cemetery Database," Vermont in the Civil War, http://vermontcivilwar.org/cem/cemetery.php; Truman Blodgett, compiled military service record.
24. Peck, *Revised Roster*, 115; Benedict, *Vermont in the Civil War*, vol. 1, 320–22; Martin Family Papers; Lewis Belknap, military pension record; *St. Albans Daily Messenger*, October 21, 1882.
25. Peck, *Revised Roster*, 114; Child, *Gazetteer of Orange County*, 519; Vermont Vital Records.

26. Peck, *Revised Roster*, 124; Vital Records, Burial Permits (1903–1905), Town Clerk's Office, Williamstown, VT, p. 1; Vermont Vital Records; Erastus Church, compiled military service and military pension records.
27. Peck, *Revised Roster*, 45, 115; Chester W. Clark, military pension record; Vermont Vital Records.
28. Peck, *Revised Roster*, 115; WPA Grave Index; John Clark, government pension application.
29. Peck, *Revised Roster*, 115; Francis B. Cosgrove, military pension record.
30. Peck, *Revised Roster*, 139.
31. Ibid., 115; WPA Grave Index.
32. Peck, *Revised Roster*, 115; WPA Grave Index; Vital Records (Marriage) Book 3, and Burial Permits, 1903–1910, Town Clerk's Office, Williamstown, VT, p. 3; *Montpelier Argus and Patriot*, October 18, 1889; *St. Albans Daily Messenger*, November 1, 1882; Frank M. Flint, compiled military service record.
33. Peck, *Revised Roster*, 115; *Montpelier Argus and Patriot*, January 11, 1905; William J. Foster, compiled military service record.
34. Peck, *Revised Roster*, 139, 758; Lydia A. George, widow's pension record.
35. Peck, *Revised Roster*, 115; John G. Green, compiled military service record.
36. Peck, *Revised Roster*, 140; Vital Records, Vol. 4 (Birth and Death) and Book 6 (Death), Town Clerk's Office, Williamstown, VT; Joseph Gregory, compiled military service record.
37. Peck, *Revised Roster*, 115, 667; *Barre Daily Times*, May 23, 1922; Vital Records, Book 8 (Death), Town Clerk's Office, Williamstown, VT, p. 127; *Vermont Phoenix*, October 2, 1862; *Montpelier Argus and Patriot*, July 31, 1886; May 2, 1889; July 24, 1889; January 12, 1898; January 24, 1900; Jason Johnson, compiled military service record.
38. Peck, *Revised Roster*, 115; *St. Albans Daily Messenger*, February 2, 1903; information from Dexter Jones's gravestone; Dexter Jones, military pension record.
39. Peck, *Revised Roster*, 115; Vital Records, Book 4 (Deaths), Town Clerk's Office, Williamstown, VT; *Executive Documents*, vol. 1, 265; Child, *Gazetteer of Orange County*, 522; information from Charles F. Lawrence's gravestone.
40. Peck, *Revised Roster*, 114; GenCircles, www.gencircles.com/users/dickott/42; Cemetery Book and Vital Records, Book 1 (Marriage), and Book 2 (Death), Town Clerk's Office, Williamstown, VT, pp. 4, 11.
41. Peck, *Revised Roster*, 114; Child, *Gazetteer of Orange County*, 160–237; Willamanna Elzy Lynde, widow's pension record; Powell, *List of Officers*, 444; *Statutes at Large*, 1231; *New York Times*, December 27, 1898.
42. Peck, *Revised Roster*, 111, 114; Child, *Gazetteer of Orange County*, 160–237; Benedict, *Vermont in the Civil War*, vol. 1, 168; Cemetery Book, Town Clerk's Office, Williamstown VT; William H. Martin, compiled military service record.
43. Peck, *Revised Roster*, 116; Eli Mayette, military pension record.
44. Peck, *Revised Roster*, 116; Dean Newcomb, compiled military service record.
45. Peck, *Revised Roster*, 116.
46. Ibid.; Frank W. Sancry, compiled military service record.
47. Peck, *Revised Roster*, 116; Child, *Gazetteer of Orange County*, 519; Henry M. Smith, compiled military service record.
48. Peck, *Revised Roster*, 132, 753; "Nationwide Gravesite Locater," United States Department of Veterans Affairs, http://gravelocator.cem.va.gov/j2ee/servlet/NGL_v1; Cross, *Melancholy Affair*, 197; William Twaddle, compiled military service record.
49. Peck, *Revised Roster*, 116, 314; Daniel G. Webster, military pension record.

50. Peck, *Revised Roster*, 116; Vital Records, Book 1B (Death), Town Clerk's Office, Williamstown, VT; Henry L. Wilson, compiled military service record.
51. Peck, *Revised Roster*, 116; Cemetery Book, Town Clerk's Office, Williamstown, VT; William C. Wilson, compiled military service record.

CHAPTER 7

52. Benedict, *Vermont in the Civil War*, 180–207.
53. Peck, *Revised Roster*, 172; James R. Martin, compiled military service record.
54. Peck, *Revised Roster*, 149, 465; Henry H. Recor, compiled military service and military pension records; Benedict, *Vermont in the Civil War*, vol. 1, 593–95; *Montpelier Argus and Patriot*, July 10, 1901; April 1, 1903; *War of the Rebellion*, vol. 45, part 1, 973; vol. 46, part 3, 1291; *Lowell Daily Citizen and News*, July 18, 1865.

CHAPTER 8

55. Benedict, *Vermont in the Civil War*, 208–33.
56. Peck, *Revised Roster*, 187; Elmer W. Boutwell, compiled military service and military pension records.
57. Peck, *Revised Roster*, 187, 648; Vital Records, Book 1 (Marriage), and Book 2 (Death), Town Clerk's Office, Williamstown, VT, pp. 7, 14; Henry Boutwell, compiled military service record.
58. Peck, *Revised Roster*, 202; Martin Family Papers; Vermont Vital Records.
59. Peck, *Revised Roster*, 184, 490; Sturtevant and Marsh, *Pictorial History*, 336, 664, 857; Orange H. Dickinson, compiled military service record; Cemetery Book and Vital Records, Burial Permits (1903–1910), Town Clerk's Office, Williamstown, VT.
60. Peck, *Revised Roster*, 187; Anna Doyle, government pension record; Benedict, *Vermont in the Civil War*, vol. 1, 366–71.
61. Peck, *Revised Roster*, 187, 399, 763; Hemenway, *Vermont Historical Gazetteer*, vol. 2, 1148; George G. Edson, compiled military service record.
62. Peck, *Revised Roster*, 200; Daniel Granger, compiled military service record.
63. Peck, *Revised Roster*, 188.
64. Ibid., 182, 203; Child, *Gazetteer of Orange County*, 160–237; Carleton, *Genealogy and Family History*, 304–5; *Montpelier Argus and Patriot*, September 24, 1890; Vital Records, Book 2 (Death), Book 4 (Death), Burial Permits 1924–30, and Cemetery Book, Town Clerk's Office, Williamstown, VT, pp. 1, 4.
65. Peck, *Revised Roster*, 188; Vermont in the Civil War, http://vermontcivilwar.org; Ancestry.com, www.ancestry.com; Cornelius McMullin, compiled military service record.
66. Peck, *Revised Roster*, 188; John O'Riley, compiled military service record; Maria S. O'Riley, veterans widow's pension application.
67. Peck, *Revised Roster*, 188, 210; Vermont in the Civil War, http://vermontcivilwar.org; Princeton University Library Digital Collections, http://diglib.princeton.edu.
68. Peck, *Revised Roster*, 195; Elijah J. Williams, compiled military service record.

CHAPTER 9

69. Benedict, *Vermont in the Civil War*, vol. 2, 1–79.
70. Peck, *Revised Roster*, 288; Nathan B. Capron, military pension application; Benedict, *Vermont in the Civil War*, vol. 2, 4–5; Vermont Vital Records.
71. Peck, *Revised Roster*, 296; Peter Duclow, military pension record.
72. Peck, *Revised Roster*, 297; WPA Grave Index; *Montpelier Argus and Patriot*, November 4, 1903; Ancestry.com, www.ancestry.com; James F. Randall, compiled military service and military pension records.

CHAPTER 10

73. Benedict, *Vermont in the Civil War*, 80–181.
74. Peck, *Revised Roster*, 87, 318; Vital Records, Book (Deaths) No. 6, Town Clerk's Office, Williamstown, VT, p. 86; Williamstown Historical Society, *History of Williamstown*, 58; John W. Bacon, military pension record; *Montpelier Argus and Patriot*, June 13, 1900; Hemenway, *Vermont Historical Gazetteer*, vol. 2, 1148.
75. Peck, *Revised Roster*, 334; Martin Family Papers; Ancestry.com, www.ancestry.com; Vital Records, Book No. 1 (Marriage), Town Clerk's Office, Williamstown, VT, p. 4; Hemenway, *Vermont Historical Gazetteer*, vol. 2, 1148; James H. Bailey, compiled military service record.
76. Peck, *Revised Roster*, 312; Ancestry.com, www.ancestry.com; *Montpelier Argus and Patriot*, October 29, 1879; Hemenway, *Vermont Historical Gazetteer*, vol. 2, 1148; James Bass, compiled military service record.
77. Peck, *Revised Roster*, 312; WPA Grave Index; "Cemetery Database," Vermont in the Civil War, http://vermontcivilwar.org/cem/cemetery.php; Ancestry.com, www.ancestry.com; Hemenway, *Vermont Historical Gazetteer*, vol. 2, 1148; Faber Benedict, compiled military service and military pension records.
78. Peck, *Revised Roster*, 319, 498; Sturtevant and Marsh, *Pictorial History*, 673; George W. Blanchard, compiled military service record.
79. Peck, *Revised Roster*, 312; WPA Grave Index; Vital Records, Book No. 2, Town Clerk's Office, Williamstown, VT, p. 9; George E. Bruce, compiled military service and military pension records.
80. Peck, *Revised Roster*, 131.
81. Ibid., 313, 498; WPA Grave Index; Sturtevant and Marsh, *Pictorial History*, 388, 677, 858; Ancestry.com, www.ancestry.com; Henry A. Dow, compiled military service and military pension records.
82. Peck, *Revised Roster*, 313, 465, 764; Ancestry.com, www.ancestry.com; Horace S. Farnham, compiled military service and military pension records; Child, *Gazetteer of Orange County*, 524.
83. Peck, *Revised Roster*, 230, 300, 310, 318, 319, 320, 756; George R. Grant, compiled military service and military pension records; Carpenter, *History of the Eighth Regiment*, 52, 298, 301; *History of Chicago, Illinois* (Chicago: Munsell & Co., 1895), available online at www.archive.org/stream/historyofchicagov2mose; Julius P. Kellogg, compiled military service and military pension records; Mary Kellogg, widow's pension application.
84. Peck, *Revised Roster*, 313; Ancestry.com, www.ancestry.com; Charles J. Green, compiled military service record.
85. Peck, *Revised Roster*, 319; WPA Grave Index; William P. Hills, compiled military service record.

86. Peck, *Revised Roster*, 313; Ullery, *Men of Vermont*, 239–40; *Williamstown Herald*, July 17, 1896; Child, *Gazetteer of Orange County*, 522; Vital Records, Deaths 1924–30, Town Clerk's Office, Williamstown, VT.
87. Peck, *Revised Roster*, 320; *Williamstown Herald*, July 17, 1896; Williamstown Historical Society, *History of Williamstown*, 275–78.
88. Peck, *Revised Roster*, 313; *Montpelier Argus and Patriot*, April 24, 1886.
89. Peck, *Revised Roster*, 313, 465; *Statutes of the United States*, 42; Vital Records, Book 6 (Death), and Cemetery Book, Town Clerk's Office, Williamstown, VT, p. 12.
90. Peck, *Revised Roster*, 314; Francis Mizer, compiled military service and military pension records.
91. Peck, *Revised Roster*, 16, 317; Child, *Gazetteer of Orange County*, 518; Charles E. Peters, compiled military service record; "Cemetery Database," Vermont in the Civil War, http://vermontcivilwar.org/cem/cemetery.php.
92. Peck, *Revised Roster*, 314; Hemenway, *Vermont Historical Gazetteer*, vol. 2, 1148; Benjamin F. Scribner, military pension record.
93. Peck, *Revised Roster*, 314, 464; Vital Records Book (Deaths), Town Clerk's Office, Williamstown, VT; Orrin Simons, compiled military service and military pension records.
94. Peck, *Revised Roster*, 327, 757; Vermont Vital Records.
95. Peck, *Revised Roster*, 314; *St. Albans Daily Messenger*, April 11, 1905; Willard G. Smith, compiled military service record.
96. Peck, *Revised Roster*, 321; Ancestry.com, www.ancestry.com; Williamstown Historical Society, *History of Williamstown*, 330–31; Vital Records, Book 6 (Deaths), Burial Permits 1876–1910 and Book II A (Deaths), Town Clerk's Office, Williamstown, VT, pp. 131, 259.
97. Peck, *Revised Roster*, 321; Ancestry.com, www.ancestry.com; "Nationwide Gravesite Locater," United States Department of Veterans Affairs, http://gravelocator.cem.va.gov/j2ee/servlet/NGL_v1; Vermont Vital Records; Francis H. Staples, compiled military service and military pension records; Wiley, *Life of Billy Yank*, 200.
98. Peck, *Revised Roster*, 321; Ancestry.com, www.ancestry.com; Milton B. Staples, compiled military service record.
99. Peck, *Revised Roster*, 116, 314; Daniel G. Webster, military pension record.
100. Peck, *Revised Roster*, 50, 314; Charles A. White, military pension record; Cemetery Book, Town Clerk's Office, Williamstown, VT.

CHAPTER 11

101. Benedict, *Vermont in the Civil War*, 182–275.
102. Peck, *Revised Roster*, 373; Cemetery Book and Vital Records, Book 3 (Deaths), Town Clerk's Office, Williamstown, VT, p. 3; Ancestry.com, www.ancestry.com; *Montpelier Argus and Patriot*, June 18, 1879; December 3, 1890; Silas B. Bohonon, military pension record.
103. Peck, *Revised Roster*, 374; "RootsWeb," Ancestry.com, http://wc.rootsweb.ancestry.com/cgi-bin/igm.cgi?op=GET&db=marston_manor&id=I4952; Vital Records, Book 2A, Town Clerk's Office, Williamstown, VT, p. 146.
104. Peck, *Revised Roster*, 374; William L. Marston, compiled military service and military pension records.
105, Peck, *Revised Roster*, 374; *Executive Documents*, vol. 1, 265; Vital Records, Burial Permits 1924–1930, Book 4 (Marriage), Town Clerk's Office, Williamstown, VT, p. 8;

Child, *Gazetteer of Orange County*, 525; *Williamstown Herald*, January 6, 1917; LaRoy S. Norris, compiled military service and military pension records.

106. Peck, *Revised Roster*, 364, 499; *Montpelier Argus and Patriot*, December 12, 1900; April 16, 1901; Vital Records, Book 2 (Deaths), and Book 4 (births and deaths), Town Clerk's Office, Williamstown, VT, p. 4; Sturtevant and Marsh, *Pictorial History*, 681–82; Charles H. Perry, military pension record.

107. Peck, *Revised Roster*, 368; Child, *Gazetteer of Orange County*, 523; Lorenzo D. Smith, compiled military service record.

CHAPTER 12

108. Benedict, *Vermont in the Civil War*, 276–341.

109. Peck, *Revised Roster*, 399; Ira J. Badger, military pension record; Vital Records, Book 2A, part 2, Town Clerk's Office, Williamstown, VT, p. 226.

110. Peck, *Revised Roster*, 399; Almon C. Boutwell, military pension record; *Rutland Daily Herald*, April 27, 1906.

111. Peck, *Revised Roster*, 399; Henry P. Burnham Papers; Burnham, *Burnham Family*, 264–65.

112. Peck, *Revised Roster*, 399; John Decamp, military pension file.

113. Peck, *Revised Roster*, 187, 399, 763; Hemenway, *Vermont Historical Gazetteer*, vol. 2, 1148.

114. Peck, *Revised Roster*, 404; Carleton, *Genealogical and Family History*, 298–99; Benedict, *Vermont in the Civil War*, vol. 2, 289–92.

115. Peck, *Revised Roster*, 399; Vital Records, Book 3 (Births and Deaths), Town Clerk's Office, Williamstown, VT.

116. Peck, *Revised Roster*, 399; Benedict, *Vermont in the Civil War*, vol. 2, 301–3; Haynes, *History of the Tenth Regiment*, 133–41; *Executive Documents*, vol. 1, 265.

117. Peck, *Revised Roster*, 400; Perry Hopkins, military pension record; *Eau Claire* [Wisconsin] *Leader*, April 11, 1914; "O'Neill Creek Cemetery," http://files.usgwarchives.org/wi/chippewa/cemeteries/oneillcrk.txt.

118. Peck, *Revised Roster*, 400, WPA Grave Index; David M. Jillson, military pension record.

119. Peck, *Revised Roster*, 400; Child, *Gazetteer of Orange County*, 530.

120. Peck, *Revised Roster*, 139; Haynes, *History of the Tenth Regiment*, 187–89; "Cemetery Database," Vermont in the Civil War, http://vermontcivilwar.org/cem/cemetery.php; Ancestry.com, www.ancestry.com; Cemetery Book, Town Clerk's Office, Williamstown, VT.

121. Peck, *Revised Roster*, 400; George L. Poor, compiled military service and military pension records; Cemetery Book, Town Clerk's Office, Williamstown, VT.

122. Peck, *Revised Roster*, 400; Vermont Vital Records; Ira A. Rice, compiled military service and military pension records.

123. Peck, *Revised Roster*, 400; Joseph K. Williams Jr., pension record; Vital Records, vol. 2A, part 2, Town Clerk's Office, Williamstown, VT, p. 256.

124. Peck, *Revised Roster*, 400; George W. Wise, military pension record.

Chapter 13

125. Benedict, *Vermont in the Civil War*, 342–96.
126. Peck, *Revised Roster*, 449; Cemetery Book, Town Clerk's Office, Williamstown, VT.
127. Peck, *Revised Roster*, 451, 467; Ancestry.com, www.ancestry.com; Barney Ring, military pension record; *Chelsea Herald*, March 22, 1900; *St. Albans Daily Messenger*, March 14, 1900; *Montpelier Argus and Patriot*, June 6, 1877; Vermont Vital Records.
128. Peck, *Revised Roster*, 444; Vital Records (Death), Book 1B, Town Clerk's Office, Williamstown, VT, p. 10; "RootsWeb," Ancestry.com, http://wc.rootsweb.ancestry.com; Genealogy.com, http://familytreemaker.genealogy.com; Edwin A. Wardwell, military pension record.

Chapter 14

129. Benedict, *Vermont in the Civil War*, 397–493.

Chapter 15

130. Benedict, *Vermont in the Civil War*, 402–5.
131. Peck, *Revised Roster*, 465; Martin Family Papers; Benedict, *Vermont in the Civil War*, vol. 2, 397, 404; Ancestry.com, www.ancestry.com; Cornelius Benedict, compiled military service record.
132. Peck, *Revised Roster*, 465; Martin Family Papers; Vital Records, Book 3 (Deaths), Book 2 (Marriages), vol. 10 (Deaths), Town Clerk's Office, Williamstown, VT, pp. 8, 14, 116; Williamstown Historical Society, *History of Williamstown*, 219–20; Child, *Gazetteer of Orange County*, 528; Orville H. Briggs, compiled military service and military pension records.
133. Peck, *Revised Roster*, 465; Find a Grave, "Henry Cram," http://www.findagrave.com/cgi-bin/fg.cgi?page=gr&GSsr=41&GSvcid=325&GRid=11381029&; "RootsWeb," Ancestry.com, http://www.rootsweb.ancestry.com/~rigenweb/Providence/article272.html; Wright, *History of Rhode Island*, 252–59; Henry Cram, compiled military service and military pension records.
134. Peck, *Revised Roster*, 19, 464; WPA Grave Index.
135. Peck, *Revised Roster*, 313, 465, 764; Ancestry.com, www.ancestry.com; Horace S. Farnham, compiled military service and military pension records; Child, *Gazetteer of Orange County*, 524.
136. Peck, *Revised Roster*, 465; Ancestry.com, www.ancestry.com; Vital Records Book 4 (Deaths), Town Clerk's Office, Williamstown, VT, p. 150.
137. Peck, *Revised Roster*, 465; Ancestry.com, www.ancestry.com; Vital Records, Book IIA, Town Clerk's Office, Williamstown, VT, p. 258.
138. Peck, *Revised Roster*, 465; Vital Records, Book 8, and Cemetery Book, Town Clerk's Office, Williamstown, VT, p. 155; Williamstown Historical Society, *History of Williamstown*, 295; Child, *Gazetteer of Orange County*, 522.
139. Peck, *Revised Roster*, 464; Henry N. Jillson Civil War Letters, Misc 743, Vermont Historical Society, Barre, VT; *Chelsea Herald*, April 20, 1900; *Montpelier Argus and Patriot*, April 25, 1900; May 2, 1900.
140. Peck, *Revised Roster*, 465; Ancestry.com, www.ancestry.com; *Executive Documents*, vol. 1, 260; Erastus E. Mann, compiled military service record.

141. Peck, *Revised Roster*, 465; Ancestry.com, www.ancestry.com.
142. Peck, *Revised Roster*, 465, 639; Ancestry.com, www.ancestry.com.
143. Peck, *Revised Roster*, 313, 465; *Statutes of the United States*, 42; Vital Records, Book 6 (Death), and Cemetery Book, Town Clerk's Office, Williamstown, VT, p. 112.
144. Peck, *Revised Roster*, 465; WPA Grave Index; "Cemetery Database," Vermont in the Civil War, http://vermontcivilwar.org/cem/cemetery.php; William A.S. McCrillis, compiled military service and military pension records.
145. Peck, *Revised Roster*, 149, 465; Henry H. Recor, military pension record; *Montpelier Argus and Patriot*, July 10, 1901; April 1, 1903; *War of the Rebellion*, vol. 45, part 1, 973; vol. 46, part 3, 1291.
146. Peck, *Revised Roster*, 451, 467; Ancestry.com, www.ancestry.com; Barney Ring, military pension record; *Chelsea Herald*, March 22, 1900; *St. Albans Daily Messenger*, March 14, 1900; *Montpelier Argus and Patriot*, June 6, 1877; Vermont Vital Records.
147. Peck, *Revised Roster*, 465; James M. Sanford, compiled military service record.
148. Peck, *Revised Roster*, 465; Ancestry.com, www.ancestry.com; James T. Seaver, compiled military service record.
149. Peck, *Revised Roster*, 465; Ancestry.com, www.ancestry.com; Vital Records (Death), Book 2, Book 10, Town Clerk's Office, Williamstown, VT, pp. 7, 73; Child, *Gazetteer of Orange County*, 523.
150. Peck, *Revised Roster*, 314, 464; Vital Records, Book (Deaths), Town Clerk's Office, Williamstown, VT; Marshall, *War of the People*, 273; Orrin Simons, compiled military service and military pension records.
151 Peck, *Revised Roster*, 466; Vital Records (Death), Book 4, Town Clerk's Office, Williamstown, VT, p. 4; Ancestry.com, www.ancestry.com; George Stebbins, military pension record; *Executive Documents*, vol. 1, 265; George Stebbins, compiled military service record.
152. Peck, *Revised Roster*, 465; Vital Records (Death), Book 8, Town Clerk's Office, Williamstown, VT, pp. 119, 151; Daniel C. Townsend, military pension record; *Montpelier Argus and Patriot*, February 26, 1890; "East Hill Cemetery, Williamstown," Townsend Tombstones, www.townsendsociety.org/Members_Only/tombstones/VT/EastHill.htm.

CHAPTER 16

153. Benedict, *Vermont in the Civil War*, 405–8.
154. Peck, *Revised Roster*, 319, 498; Sturtevant and Marsh, *Pictorial History*, 673; George W. Blanchard, compiled military service record.
155. Peck, *Revised Roster*, 184, 490; Sturtevant and Marsh, *Pictorial History*, 336, 664, 857; Orange H. Dickinson, compiled military service record; Cemetery Book and Vital Records, Burial Permits (1903–1910), Town Clerk's Office, Williamstown, VT.
156. Peck, *Revised Roster*, 313, 498; WPA Grave Index; Sturtevant and Marsh, *Pictorial History*, 388, 677, 858; Ancestry.com, www.ancestry.com; Henry A. Dow, military pension record.
157. Peck, *Revised Roster*, 497; Ancesrty.com, www.ancestry.com; Sturtevant and Marsh, *Pictorial History*, 336, 664, 857; Child, *Gazetteer of Orange County*, 521; Vital Records, Book 6 (Deaths), and Book 7 (Deaths), Town Clerk's Office, Williamstown, VT, pp. 78, 96; George W. Nichols, compiled military service and military pension records.
158. Peck, *Revised Roster*, 364, 499; *Montpelier Argus and Patriot*, December 12, 1900; April 16, 1901; Sturtevant and Marsh, *Pictorial History*, 681–82; Charles H. Perry, military pension record.

159. Peck, *Revised Roster*, 490; Sturtevant and Marsh, *Pictorial History*, 536, 849; Vital Records, Book 8 (Deaths), Town Clerk's Office, Williamstown, VT, pp. 13, 76; Joseph A. Sanders, military pension record.

CHAPTER 17

160. Peck, *Revised Roster*, 516; Samuel B. Rice, compiled military service record.

CHAPTER 18

161. Benedict, *Vermont in the Civil War*, 411–13.
162. Peck, *Revised Roster*, 553; Cemetery Book, Town Clerk's Office, Williamstown, VT; Heman G. Perry, compiled military service and military pension records.
163. Peck, *Revised Roster*, 533; Vermont Vital Records.

CHAPTER 19

164. Benedict, *Vermont in the Civil War*, 496–532.
165. Peck, *Revised Roster*, 586, 759; Francis F. Parmenter, compiled military service record; Gilman Parmenter, dependent father's pension record.
166. Peck, *Revised Roster*, 594; Vital Records, Book 2B, Town Clerk's Office, Williamstown, VT, p. 3.

CHAPTER 20

167. Benedict, *Vermont in the Civil War*, 533–695.
168. Peck, *Revised Roster*, 255; Vital Records, Book 5 (Death), and Book 8 (Death), Town Clerk's Office, Williamstown, VT, pp. 1, 146.
169. Peck, *Revised Roster*, 233; Vital Record, Book 5 (Death), and Cemetery Book, Town Clerk's Office, Williamstown, VT, p. 47; L. Baxter Richardson, compiled military service record.
170. Peck, *Revised Roster*, 233; William F. Ring, military pension record.
171. Peck, *Revised Roster*, 233; Williamstown Historical Society, *History of Williamstown*, 328; *Barre Daily Times*, May 18, 1919; Vital Records (Death), Book 3, Book 2, Book 8, Town Clerk's Office, Williamstown, VT, pp. 2, 45; Vermont Vital Records; George W. Savery, compiled military service record; Savery genealogy information provided by Kristin Hallett.
172. Peck, *Revised Roster*, 233; Vital Records (Death), Book 5, and Book 6, Town Clerk's Office, Williamstown, VT, pp. 22, 68; Child, *Gazetteer of Orange County*, 526–27; Cross, *Melancholy Affair*, 198; Gilbert O. Smith, compiled military service and military pension records; undated clipping from the *Randolph Herald*.

CHAPTER 21

173. Benedict, *Vermont in the Civil War*, 732–53.
174. Peck, *Revised Roster*, 19, 601; Martin Family Papers; Benedict, *Vermont in the Civil War*, vol. 2, 731–33; Ai Brown, compiled military service record.

CHAPTER 22

175. Benedict, *Vermont in the Civil War*, 710–19.
176. Peck, *Revised Roster*, 637, 653; Child, *Gazetteer of Orange County*, 529; Cemetery Book, Town Clerk's Office, Williamstown, VT; Ancestry.com, www.ancestry.com; Charles J. Cram, military pension record.
177. Peck, *Revised Roster*, 465, 639; Ancestry.com, www.ancestry.com.

CHAPTER 23

178. Benedict, *Vermont in the Civil War*, 720–30.
179. Peck, *Revised Roster*, 187, 648; Vital Records Book 1 (Marriage), and Book 2 (Death), Town Clerk's Office, Williamstown, VT, pp. 7, 14.
180. Peck, *Revised Roster*, 650.

CHAPTER 24

181. Benedict, *Vermont in the Civil War*, 717–18.
182. Peck, *Revised Roster*, 637, 653; Child, *Gazetteer of Orange County*, 529; Ancestry.com, www.ancestry.com; Vital Records (Death), Book 8, Book 7, Town Clerk's Office, Williamstown, VT, pp. 84, 149; Charles J. Cram, military pension record.

CHAPTER 25

183. Boatner, *Civil War Dictionary*, 870.
184. Peck, *Revised Roster*, 115, 667; *Barre Daily Times*, May 23, 1922; Vital Records, Book 8 (Death), Town Clerk's Office, Williamstown, VT, p. 127; *Vermont Phoenix*, October 2, 1862; *Montpelier Argus and Patriot*, July 31, 1886; May 2, 1889; July 24, 1889; January 12, 1898; January 24, 1900.

CHAPTER 26

185. Peck, *Revised Roster*, 670; Hemenway, *Vermont Historical Gazetteer*, vol. 2, 1148.
186. Peck, *Revised Roster*, 671; Vital Records, Book 4 (Death), vol. 5, Town Clerk's Office, Williamstown, VT, p. 4.

CHAPTER 27

187. Peck, *Revised Roster*, 114; Child, *Gazetteer of Orange County*, 160–237; Willamanna Elzy Lynde, widow's pension record; Powell, *List of Officers*, 444; *Statutes at Large*, vol. 32, part 2, 1231; *New York Times*, December 27, 1898.
188. Peck, *Revised Roster*, 680; Wadsworth, *Incident at San Augustine Springs*, 9–364; Vital Records, Book 2A, Town Clerk's Office, Williamstown, VT; *Barre-Montpelier Times Argus*, September 21, 2009; Gerald A. Hinckley to Senator Patrick Leahy, letter, June 20, 2009; Katherine Long to Gerald A. Hinckley, letter, July 1, 2009; Colonel Michael S. Yarmie to Gerald A. Hinckley, letter, August 10, 2009; Warner, *Generals in Blue*, 119.
189. Peck, *Revised Roster*, 681; Ellis, *Norwich University*, 718.

CHAPTER 28

190. Vermont Free Public Library Service, *Vermont Libraries*, 68; Stennett, *History of Place Names*, 12; Lurton, *Iowa and the Rebellion*, 182; Merry, *History of Delaware County*, 103; Ellis, *Norwich University*, 718.
191. Hogle and Beckett, *Beckett Family History*, 37–45; Andrew W. Beckett, compiled military service and military pension records.
192. Hemenway, *Vermont Historical Gazetteer*, vol. 2, 192; Ancestry.com, www.ancestry.com; *Catalogue of the Officers*, 14; Eddy, *Patriotism of Illinois*, 76–77; Isaac L. Clark, compiled military service record.
193. Vermont in the Civil War, http://vermontcivilwar.org/index.php; "John Coughlin," Arlington National Cemetery Website, http://www.arlingtoncemetery.net/jcoughli.htm; Ayling, *Revised Register*, 524.
194. *Williamstown Herald*, June 17, 1896; Vital Records, Book 7 (Death), Town Clerk's Office, Williamstown, VT, p. 31; John Lynde, compiled military service and military pension records.
195. Vital Records, Book 3 (Death), Town Clerk's Office, Williamstown, VT, p. 2; Joseph B. Norris, compiled military service and military pension records.
196. Vermont in the Civil War, http://vermontcivilwar.org/index.php; Ayling, *Revised Register*, 917.
197. George F. Taplin, compiled military service and military pension records.
198. Cemetery Book, Town Clerk's Office, Williamstown, VT; George H. Watson, compiled military service record.

CHAPTER 29

199. Peck, *Revised Roster*, 700.
200. Ibid., 702.
201. Ibid., 704.

CHAPTER 30

202. Ibid., 55, 240; *Barre Daily Times*, June 4, 1929; June 24 and 25, 1931; Vital Records Book 10 (Death), Town Clerk's Office, Williamstown, VT, p. 15; Charles I. Preston, military pension record.

BIBLIOGRAPHY

Published Primary Sources

Peck, Theodore S. *Revised Roster of Vermont Volunteers and Lists of Vermonters Who Served in the Army and Navy of the United States During the War of the Rebellion, 1861–66*. Montpelier, VT: Watchman Co., 1892.

Manuscripts

Burnham, Henry P., Papers, MSB 30. Vermont Historical Society, Barre, VT.

Jillson, Henry, Civil War Letters, MISC 743. Vermont Historical Society, Barre, VT.

Martin Family Papers, MISC 873. Vermont Historical Society, Barre, VT.

General Works

Ayling, Augustus D. *Revised Register of the Soldiers and Sailors of New Hampshire in the War of the Rebellion 1861–1866*. Concord, NH: Ira C. Evans, Public Printer, 1895.

Benedict, George G. *Vermont in the Civil War: A History of the Part Taken by the Vermont Soldiers and Sailors in the War for the Union, 1861–5*. 2 vols. Burlington, VT: Free Press Association, 1886 and 1888.

Boatner, Mark M., III. *The Civil War Dictionary*. New York: Vintage Civil War Library, 1991.

Burnham, Roderick H. *The Burnham Family; of Genealogical Records of the Decedents of the Four Emigrants of the Name, Who Were Among the Early Settlers in America*. Hartford, CT: Press of Case, Lockwood & Brainard, 1869.

Carlton, Hiram. *Genealogical and Family History of the State of Vermont*. 2 vols. New York: Lewis Publishing Co., 1903.

Carpenter, George N. *History of the Eighth Regiment Vermont Volunteers, 1861–1865*. Boston: Press of Deland & Barta, 1886.

Catalogue of the Officers and Students of Dartmouth College for the Academic Year 1845–6. Hanover, NH: Printed at the Dartmouth Press, 1845.

Child, Hamilton, comp. *Gazetteer of Orange County, Vt., 1762–1888.* Part 1. Syracuse, NY: Syracuse Journal Company, Printers, 1888.

Cross, David Faris. *A Melancholy Affair at the Weldon Railroad.* Shippensburg, PA: White Mane Books, 2003.

Eddy, Thomas Mears. *The Patriotism of Illinois: A Record of the Civil and Military History of the State in the War for the Union, With a History of the Campaigns in Which Illinois Soldiers have Been Conspicuous, Sketches of Distinguished Officers, the Roll of the Illustrious Dead, Movements of the Sanitary and Christian Commissions.* Chicago: Clarke and Co., 1866.

Ellis, William A., ed. *Norwich University, 1819–1911: Her History, Her Graduates, Her Roll of Honor, Published by Major-General Grenville M. Dodge.* 3 vols. Compiled and edited by William Arba Ellis. Montpelier, VT: Capitol City Press, 1911.

Haynes, E.M. *A History of the Tenth Regiment, Vt. Vols. with Biographical Sketches.* Rutland, VT: Tuttle Company, Printers, 1894.

Hemenway, Abby Maria. *The Vermont Historical Gazetteer: A Magazine, Embracing a History of Each Town, Civil, Ecclesiastical, Biographical and Military.* 5 vols. Burlington, VT: Tuttle Co., 1923.

Hogle, Emily Beckett, and Merrill A. Beckett, comps. *Beckett Family History.* N.p., n.d.

Lurton, Dunham Ingersoll. *Iowa and the Rebellion.* Philadelphia: J.B. Lippincott and Co., 1867.

Marshall, Jeffrey D. *A War of the People.* Hanover, NH: University Press of New England, 1999.

Merry, John F. *History of Delaware County, Iowa, and Its People.* Chicago: S.J. Clarke Publishing Company, 1914.

Powell, William H., comp. *List of Officers of the Army of the United States from 1779 to 1900, Embracing a Register of all appointments by the President of the United States in the Volunteer Service during the Civil War and of Volunteer Officers in the Service of the United States June 1, 1900.* New York: L.R. Hamersly & Co., 1900.

Stennett, William H., comp. *A History of the Origin of the Place Names Connected with the Chicago & North Western and Chicago, St. Paul, Minneapolis & Omaha Railways.* Chicago, 1908.

Sturtevant, Ralph Orson, and Carmi Lathrop Marsh. *Pictorial History: Thirteenth Regiment Vermont Volunteers, War of 1861–1865.* N.p., 1910.

Ullery, Jacob G., comp. *Men of Vermont: Illustrated Biographical History of Vermonters & Sons of Vermont.* Brattleboro, VT: Transcript Publishing Company, 1894.

Vermont Free Public Library Service. *Vermont Libraries: Biennial Report of the Free Public Library Service.* N.p.: Vermont Free Public Library Commission, Vermont Free Public Library Dept., 1912.

Wadsworth, Richard. *Incident at San Augustine Springs: A Hearing for Major Isaac Lynde.* Las Cruces, NM: Yucca Tree Press, 2002.

Warner, Ezra J. *Generals in Blue: Lives of the Union Commanders.* Baton Rouge: Louisiana State University Press, 1964.

Washington Government Printing Office. *The Executive Documents Printed by the Order of the Senate of the United States for the Second Session of the Forty-Seventh Congress, 1882–1883.* 5 vols. Washington, D.C.: Government Printing Office, 1883.

———. *The Statutes at Large of the United States of America, From December, 1901, to March, 1903, Concurrent Resolutions of the Two Houses of Congress, and Recent Treaties, Conventions, and Executive Proclamations.* Washington, D.C.: Government Printing Office, 1903.

———. *Statutes of the United States of America, Passed at the Second Session of the Fifty-Fifth Congress 1897–1898*. Washington, D.C.: Government Printing Office, 1898.———. *War of the Rebellion: A Compilation of the Official Records of the Union and Confederate Armies*. Washington, D.C.: Government Printing Office, 1902.

Wiley, Bell Irvin. *The Life of Billy Yank: The Common Soldier of the Union*. Baton Rouge: Louisiana State University Press, 1978.

Williamstown Historical Society. *A History of Williamstown, Vermont, 1781–1991*. N.p., 1991.

Wright, Albert J. *History of the State of Rhode Island with Illustrations*. Philadelphia: Hong, Wade & Co., 1878.

Zeller, Paul G. *The Second Vermont Volunteer Infantry Regiment, 1861–1865*. Jefferson, NC: McFarland & Co. Publisher, Inc., 2002.

NEWSPAPERS

Barre Daily Times
Barre-Montpelier Times Argus
Lowell Daily Citizen and News
Montpelier Argus and Patriot
St. Albans Daily Messenger

INDEX

A

B

C

D

T

V

W

ABOUT THE AUTHOR

Paul Zeller is a retired colonel in the U.S. Army Reserve and previously worked as a chief of training development for the U.S. Army Transportation Corps. He is a member of the Williamstown Historical Society, a volunteer at the Vermont Historical Society, president of the Friends of the Ainsworth Public Library in Williamstown, a member of the Williamstown Planning Commission and a Williamstown Cemetery commissioner. He was nominated to revise the Williamstown historical society's town history in the fall of 2008 and is the author of *The Second Vermont Infantry Regiment, 1861–1865* (McFarland & Co., 2002) and *The Ninth Vermont Infantry: A History and Roster* (McFarland & Co., 2008). His published articles include: "Sleeping Before the Fire," *Military Images* (2006); "Supplying an Army," *History Connections* (Vermont Historical Society, Spring 2008); "Civil War Humor," *History Connections* (Vermont Historical Society, Summer 2008); and "Deceit or Valor? One Vermont Family's Decision During the Civil War," *History Connections* (Vermont Historical Society, Winter 2009).